COWBOYS & COCKTAILS

My Adventurous Gap Year in Warsaw

By Ellie LaCrosse

Published by The Book Chief Publishing House 2022
Suite 2A, Blackthorn House, St Paul's Square, Birmingham, B3 1RL
www.thebookchief.com

The moral right of the authors have been asserted.

Text Copyright 2022 by **Ellie LaCrosse**

All rights reserved. No part of this book may be reproduced, stored in a retrieval system, or transmitted in any form or by any means, electronic, mechanical, photocopying, recording, public performances or otherwise, without written permission of **Ellie LaCrosse**, except for brief quotations embodied in critical articles or reviews. The book is for personal and commercial use and has been agreed by the author.

The right of **Ellie LaCrosse** to be identified as the author of this work has been asserted in accordance with sections 77 and 78 of the copyright Designs and Patents Act 1988.

Book Cover Design: Deearo Marketing
Editor: Laura Billingham
Typesetting: Nicola Matthews
Publishing: Sharon Brown

THE BOOK CHIEF
IGNITE YOUR WRITING

Table of Contents

Dedication 9
Acknowledgements 11
Introduction 13
Prologue 17
CHAPTER 1 23
   A Phone Call 23
CHAPTER 2 45
   Homework 45
CHAPTER 3 55
   Saying Goodbye 55
CHAPTER 4 69
   Coach Traveller 69
CHAPTER 5 81
   Early Days 81
CHAPTER 6 93
   Introductions & Misunderstandings 93
CHAPTER 7 109
   Flat Hunting 109
CHAPTER 8 119
   Vodka & Y2K Malarky 119
CHAPTER 9 127
   Cowboys 127
CHAPTER 10 135
   Cocktails 135
CHAPTER 11 149
   Sexual Healing 149

CHAPTER 12	181
The Korma Incident	**181**
CHAPTER 13	187
Serendipity	**187**
CHAPTER 14	201
Exploration	**201**
CHAPTER 15	209
Rose-Tinted Romance	**209**
CHAPTER 16	217
Polish Tooth Fairy	**217**
CHAPTER 17	229
Chopin Festival	**229**
CHAPTER 18	237
Visa Dramas	**237**
CHAPTER 19	251
Domestika	**251**
CHAPTER 20	263
Details	**263**
Conclusion	275
About the Author	279

'The first step towards getting somewhere is to decide you're not going to stay where you are.'

J. P. Morgan

Dedication

To Gary, the best of the bunch. I love you x

Acknowledgements

To my Parents, I'll always be grateful for the opportunity you gave me to find some space to think through how I was going to put my life back together again after my first divorce.

I know you were often baffled by my decisions, but you gave me unconditional love and support.

To my beautiful Daughter, I hope in the telling of my story, you can fill in some of the missing gaps, and you can forgive me for being so far away when you missed me. You were always in my thoughts daily.

Ad Astra Per Aspera.

Introduction

I love telling stories. Especially stories about my life. At nearly sixty years of age, I've enough material to write several books about my roller-coaster life!

The book is aimed at anyone who's been through a painful break-up in their relationship, especially in middle-age. Just when you are expected to stop sowing wild oats and living like a perpetual student and settle down to produce the next generation.

For anyone that has felt ripped to shreds emotionally, is numb with grief and has been financially cleaned out, I want this book to spark a smile of recognition and a little sprinkling of re-discovering the identity of the 'you' before the catastrophes of life, and the vagaries of experience knock your self-esteem.

Rediscover what sparked joy and passions in your life, and be brave enough to grab new adventures, as a way of breaking down the walls we often build around our hearts to protect us from being hurt or used again.

I like to think I have a wry sense of humour that has got me out of tight spots in my past, and kept the kernel of hope alive in my soul when I felt utterly lost and vulnerable. It's part of my authorial 'voice' and I'm no longer apologising for being authentically myself through my writing style.

"Why did you have to go all the way to Poland?"

This was a familiar refrain within my family. I went because I'd been fascinated with the country ever since my university days of studying the political systems of Eastern Europe, and those political systems that are no longer relevant, such as Communism and Stalinism. Plus, I was oddly intrigued by World War II.

There was a sizeable Polish population in my home city of Peterborough, and I'd always liked listening to stories about the Warsaw Uprising of 1944 from a delicatessen shop owner near where I lived. He brought to life the epic struggles for freedom, and I just formed an opinion that the Polish people were to be admired for their grit and gumption.

This book is NOT a travelogue of Poland or Warsaw. When I left the UK in 1999 to take up a teaching contract, most people, including members of my own family, were non-plussed as to why I wanted to visit (in their eyes) a slightly unknown, ex-Soviet satellite state in Eastern Europe.

So, many years later, after my first divorce, when I was a struggling single parent being given a unique chance to work in Poland and Warsaw, I grabbed it. In addition, it was an extraordinary opportunity and took me as far away from my comfort zone as I could imagine to help heal my past.

I wanted to return to the Ellie before the drip-drip, soul-destroying clipping away of my self-esteem and, if I'm perfectly honest, the sheer boredom of a dry, uninteresting, and prescribed marriage. I was simply too young to have really matured and developed as a fully rounded individual knowing my strengths and failings.

Writing this memoir has given me the opportunity to review this brief episode in my life with the benefit of the long lens of hindsight. I've had several aha moments when I was reviewing my life actions and their consequences, like looking at a film screen in my head. Once I was in the full flow of the writing process, whole chunks of conversations just wrote themselves on the page. Whilst memory isn't always totally reliable, or totally accurate, some conversations have been seared into my long-term memory.

At times, it's been uncomfortable to re-live buried painful memories, and I sought some self-care after I completed my draft. It felt like closure and was cathartic for me.

This memoir is MY version of MY story about MY life during the late 1990s. However, I hope it inspires others to realise that life is a funny old game, and if you're courageous enough to break the Status Quo, you too could find unexpected happiness and adventures you didn't know you were capable of experiencing.

Ellie.

'There is no greater agony than bearing an untold story inside you.' (Maya Angelou)

Prologue

I knew the exact moment when I felt the wrench of separation, home, daughter, life, country. In fact, everything I thought I understood about my life to date. I was a middle-aged woman on a ferry leaving the Port of Dover.

I glanced over my shoulder, sitting in the ferry cafe, looking through the bright, gleaming panes of glass to the famous White Cliffs. I blinked as a rising sob got stuck in my tightening throat. The cliffs looked like a huge smile of pearly white teeth, benignly smiling at me a cheery Bon Voyage!

I couldn't believe how emotional I felt. The previous six months of preparation, sorting out Visas, arranging new schools, the general upheaval and the bewildered looks on my parent's and crumbled angelic face of my beloved daughter. I felt vulnerable. I had wanted a fresh start, a chance to clear the slate and wipe away the emotional debris of a heart-breaking and traumatic divorce from my ex-husband, the father of my daughter.

Travelling to the Continent on a shoestring budget, mid-Winter was a life experience not to be repeated.

After thirty-five hours on a transcontinental coach, finally arriving at a cold coach station in the centre of Warsaw was like arriving on a frozen new plant. So alien to me, that for the first few minutes after collecting my large, heavy suitcase, I was rooted in the 'fight or flight' stress mode, constantly swivelling my head, trying to gain a familiar bearing.

My logical, survival instincts kicked in, and I reached into my pocket for my trusty phrasebook. I'd been practicing stock phrases the entire duration of the trip. There was a brief moment of victory when I applied my new 'proficiency' in Polish. I'd spotted a tatty kiosk with a flashing neon Herbata word on a rotating light stand in the central concourse.

I approached shyly and asked for a herbata (tea) and pointed with my finger (the Universal language of the traveller), and a polystyrene cup of steaming black tea was produced.

"Hurrah!"

I felt immediately calmer and comforted. I had used foreign currency and asked for a drink. I wouldn't die of thirst at least!

I was supported by the Language School I'd been contracted to work with, and life quickly evolved from survival to flat-hunting and enjoying my new lifestyle as an ex-pat.

My students were not children but adult language learners from the world of corporate business, large multinational firms with a highly trained, managerial or technically skilled workforce.

They were always amused at how 'English' I would appear to them, carrying my trusty telescopic brolly in my bag at all times, even though the weather was solidly Continental with definite seasons and hardly rained. Perhaps a short, sharp downpour in the spring, but the transition from bitterly cold winters to swelteringly hot summers was a swift one.

Teaching English to adults was always full of fun and pitfalls. Interestingly, I could guarantee rapt attention for all of my unscripted lessons by using fruity or weird colloquialisms. Then the class would erupt with chortling, sniggering, and knowing glances exchanged as if they were a class of infants.

I vividly remember a lesson I was supposed to deliver to a bunch of highly trained mechanics at a large motor manufacturer on the outskirts of Warsaw. The sprawling factory was based on a floodplain by the mighty River Vistula, a godforsaken bleak backwater.

On this ordinary day, I was expecting a group of around eight to ten. However, one of the school Secretaries had double-booked the session, and I walked into a fairly noisy, sweaty, crowded room with approximately thirty adult students.

Frankly, I was a little overwhelmed with this introduction, so I whipped out of my trusty briefcase a 'Plan B' lesson plan. It always saved my arse in tense situations and was all about British food idioms.

The quirkiness and arcane rules of vocabulary and grammar never cease to amaze me, and English idioms never ceased to confuse my students! The food idiom, 'Toad-in-the-hole' or 'Pigs-in-blankets' is understood by most native British English speakers to mean a dish of sausages covered in batter.

However, a wag in my class suddenly stood up and asked, "Can I say pork-in-a-hole or pork-in-the-blanket?"

I shot out of my seat and waved my hand furiously around my face, "No! No, absolutely NOT!" I screeched, "Not unless you want your face slapped!"

There then arose a labyrinthine explanation vis-a-vis the British sense of humour. Much merriment ensued.

Hilariously, as feedback forms were returned from the car manufacturer to my bosses at the language school a week or two later, my immediate manager was bemused to read out at the weekly staff-meeting.

"We especially enjoyed Pana Ella's sex-talk about food. We learnt a lot about 'Pork-in-the-bed'."

CENTRAL WARSAW

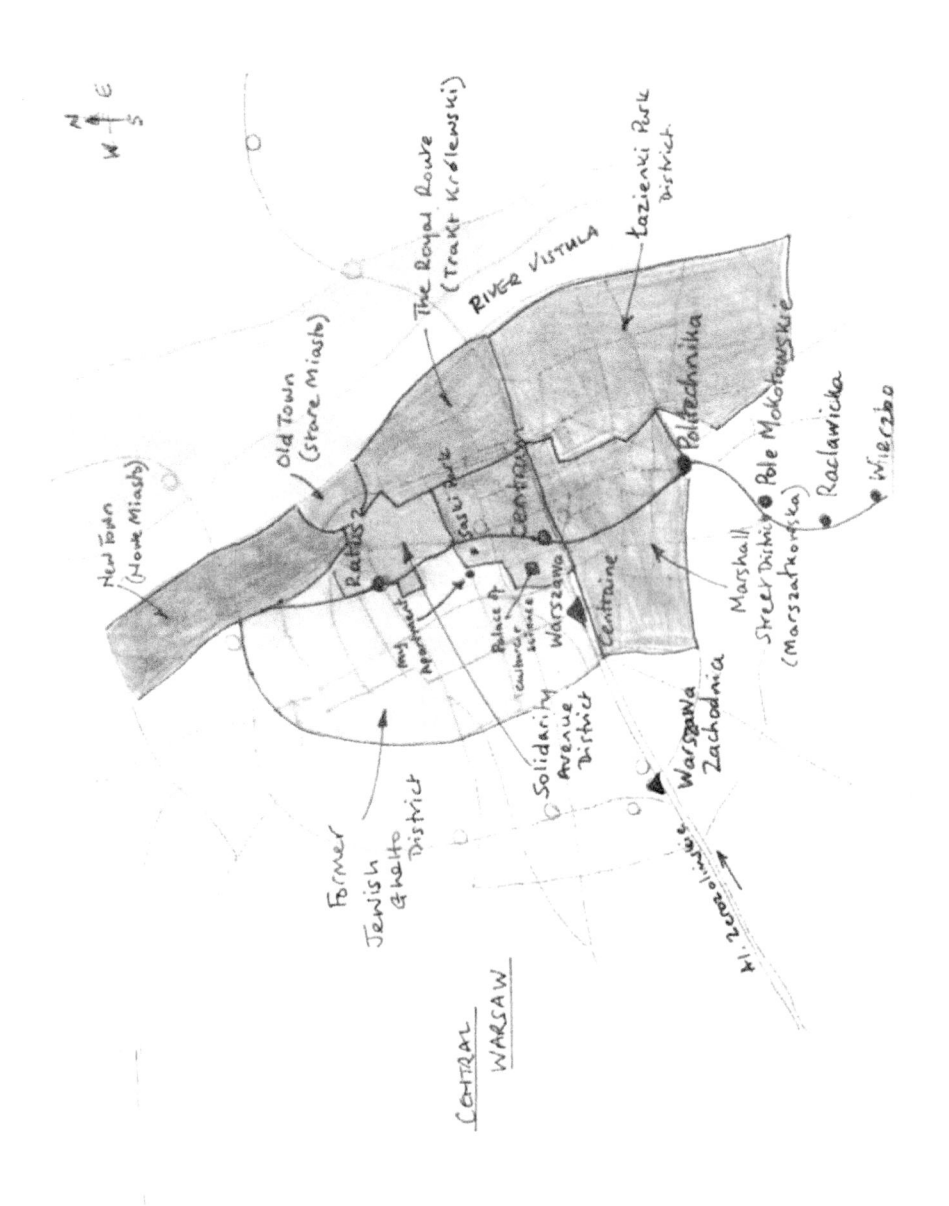

CHAPTER 1

A Phone Call

If anyone had said to me at the start of the year in 1998 that later that year, I would have been making plans to work overseas and that by early 1999, I was literally packing a case and making last-minute preparations to set off on a new adventure, I would have thought they were a sandwich short of a picnic!

A casual observer of my life at that time, would have assumed I had a successful career in business and that my daughter was thriving at school. Delving deeper and peering into the darker recesses would have revealed a slightly different picture. I was recently divorced from my daughter's father. Emotionally, I was a fully functioning wreck.

I was like an iceberg emotionally, cold, floating, solid, but four-fifths of me was drowning under the surface. A swirling, hidden mess of disintegrating neurosis and guilt.

No-one really understood the inner turmoil and loneliness I was experiencing. I didn't want people to get close enough to see how deeply unrooted I felt. My daughter was too young to understand, and at the time, my parents were too far away to do much to help day-to-day.

Her Dad had been a decent, kind chap. I had loved him deeply at the start of our relationship at Aston University, where we had met during the early 1980s. I thought he was the most handsome man I'd clapped eyes on. Our initial meeting was at my 21st birthday bash in a Birmingham nightclub. I was dating another boyfriend at the time; however, we had noticed each other.

Months later, after my short-lived romance with the other guy fizzled out, mutual friends could see our attraction and conspired to see us get together. Over the next few years, we got married, forged ahead with our careers, and I thought we were happy together.

Then the vagaries of life, money stresses, childbirth, meddling by his over-protective mother and differing personalities started to bring cracks and tensions into the once happy home-life.

After a few more years, I realised my husband and I were very different characters and were making each other very unhappy. I had an affair. Happy people don't have affairs. I was like a drowning woman, clinging onto a raft for the first man that would show some attention to me. My Ex could not find it in himself to open up emotionally; he could never really talk to me, and even though I'd begged and begged to seek couples counselling, he flatly refused. I craved the intimacy of sharing my intellect, creativity, hopes and fears with another.

Even when we decided, for the sake of our daughter, to try to salvage our relationship, my Ex acknowledged he had neglected me emotionally, which had been a contributing factor in the initial separation.

I returned to him, but I felt like I was walking on eggshells for several months. Nothing had really changed about our dynamic, and when I finally called time on the relationship, it was a brutal parting. I thought all the love had died. It was still there however, tucked away in a corner of my heart, and I spent months and months and months silently grieving for what we'd had and then lost.

It seemed to me that I was in a permanent state of anxiety after my eventual divorce. The tyranny of shouldering the burden of parenting, domestic chores and holding down a responsible professional career was starting to take its toll on my health.

My weight ballooned over this period. The usual habit of a little tipple before retiring for the night, insidiously escalated to drinking a glass of wine as soon as I entered my kitchen after work. One or two glasses over dinner sipped slowly, then more grazing mindlessly with snacks in front of the TV, yet more wine swilled down before, near oblivion, I made my way to my lonely bed.

I was highly functioning. I always made sure my daughter was clean, tidy, and ate well. I invested time in story reading and ensuring she felt protected, comfortable and safe.

The hamster wheel of existence trundled on and on for many months. I was grief-stricken over my divorce. I had unresolved feelings of guilt. I had a ton of judgement from family for having caused the divorce, although no one had counselled either of us, sat us down and got to the root causes. No one ever considered my point of view; no one ever said to my ex, "What was your part in this tragedy?" He always had my family's support, never sanction, and the injustice burned deep within me, creating my very low self-esteem.

My family had memories of me during this period, being grumpy, sensitive, tetchy. I was short-tempered with work colleagues and sometimes snappy with my darling girl. Which would often make me feel like a worthless, discarded rag doll, all the stuffing knocked out of her.

So, I was a broken, raging, middle-aged, single mother.

I'd always tried my best to be a good mother to my daughter to the best of my ability and budget. Shockingly, I did consider suicide on more than one occasion during this period. Depressingly, I realised when I was arranging Life Insurance, that I was worth more dead than alive. At my lowest, the single thought of how my daughter would have had to cope with that burden, always, always stopped me in my tracks.

Thank God for The Samaritans. That wonderful service, with anonymous, kind, empathetic voices, at the end of a life-line telephone call, literally saved my sanity and, I think, my life.

I look back and feel ashamed to admit it, but in telling my story, it's important to understand my why. Why I felt compelled to want to clean the slate and move past this sad episode of my life. It has also given me compassion for others I've met in my life, dealing with their own trauma.

Frankly, at this time, I was numb. Life was flowing on, and I really wasn't engaged with it. I was on autopilot, work, drinking, parenting, work, drinking, parenting. Music helped. One of my passions in life is listening to all sorts of music. Another is the cinema.

I kept up this parallel-universe appearance when I'd hand my girl over to her dad every two weeks at some motorway services, roughly mid-way to where we'd be living at the time.

Thankfully, her dad and I, whilst not friends, did respect the fact we were life-long parents. We muddled through the arrangements with a modicum of civility, and I never, ever, stopped my daughter from seeing her dad.

I'm sure many separated and divorced couples can relate to the 'hand-over-child-at-a-car-park-off-a-motorway-with-lots-of-bags' scenario. A quick exchange, checking there were enough clean pants and books packed. A final hug, a peck on the cheek, a cheery wave goodbye. Then a misty-eyed lump in the throat feeling as the one perfect thing in your life was whisked away and disappeared from view.

This was quickly followed by a brief quickening of the pulse and rising excitement that the stopwatch of weekend freedom had started the countdown. Go! Go! Go!

However, the promise of a child-free weekend rarely lived up to expectations. By the time I had rushed around doing the domestic catch-up, paying bills, shopping for supplies, re-stocking the fridge and freezer and tackling the epic laundry mountain, my solitary Saturday was over.

Sometimes, I'd sign up to dating sites and have an hour or two flirting online (pre-Tinder) just to have some connection and chat with another human. I didn't rush out to go boozing in bars or to clubs. Firstly, I'm a little old-fashioned, and secondly, I'm really quite shy, so I'd occasionally go onto telephone dating sites to just have 'contact' with people, mostly men. Just to talk, flirt and very occasionally hook-up for no-strings sex.

It temporarily made me feel alive.

The feelings didn't last more than a few fleeting hours. It was like a very unsatisfying snack, not sustaining. No true intimacy, as the heart-wall I'd built up brick by brick was firmly in place, and each time, a sliver of my glass-like pride was crushed underfoot, and another brick was added to that wall of defence.

Sundays were always my favourite day of the weekend. If my daughter was home, we'd try and do something fun or go somewhere together, even if it was only shopping.

I remember vividly one Sunday when we went to Leeds to shop for new clothes. After spending most of the time traipsing around shops looking for bright, sparkly girl-crap that the average six-year-old could empty their pocket money on, my arms were weighed down with all the bags, my handbag and a child's hand. My poor back!

After the obligatory happy meal at McD's, it was finally my turn to shop. This shop was for new underwear. It usually meant a quick scurry around M&S; however, on this occasion, it turned into one of the most humiliatingly funny incidents of my life.

I needed some new sturdy, no-nonsense pants, the sort M&S are rightly famous for. M&S, for reasons only known to themselves, had elected to change the sizing on the hangers since my last pant shop. They had grouped sizes together, and I found that I needed to go up a size (nothing to do with me having piled on the pounds by grazing on crisps and quaffing too much wine).

As I began lifting the pants on the hangers up to inspect, my daughter blurted out, a little too loudly, "Oh, Mum! They look like parachutes!"

Not only did every head swivel around to look in my direction, but just in case no-one had heard the first time, she bellowed, "Parachutes! Your bum is like a parachute!"

"Be quiet darling!" I replied, in vain.

"But, your bum is big mum; when you bend down you block out the light!" she giggled.

There's nothing like the searing honesty of a six-year-old, is there? So, in subsequent years, if I asked for my girl's opinion on my choice of attire and asked the question, 'Does my bum look big in this?'
I knew she'd say yes!

The Sunday matinee at the cinema was my guilty pleasure. I admit I'm a film buff. I adore Arthouse, Foreign language, Film-Noir, Horror, Thrillers, Comedies. In fact, all genres except Sci-Fi and Zombie Apocalypse!

There's a certain smell inside a cinema, a reek of sweat, sugar and sex. The sensory overload of the big-screen experience was what I loved about it. I could gaze up and be transported out of my hamster wheel drudgery for two hours. I wouldn't have to think about being sad and miserable. It was a sort of therapy.

The phone call came during the middle of one of my home-alone weekends. My daughter was spending time with her dad, and I had just returned home from the cinema. I nearly missed the call, so I was a little breathless when I answered.

The phone-line crackled a bit - I still used a landline in those days:

"Hello! Ellie? Ells! It's Steph! How are you?" Steph breezed.

"Steph? Steph? What on earth? I haven't spoken to you for years! What is it four, five years? Blast from the past, Mrs…so what do I owe the honour of a call?" I teased.

Steph had been a pal of mine from Uni days. We had been good friends; we were on the same degree course. We had shared squalid digs together in a shabby part of Birmingham before I got together with my daughter's dad.

She was an irrepressible force-of-nature. Madcap. Northern. Loud. For the first few years after graduation, we'd kept in touch regularly, but then life got in the way, and we lost contact.

"I know, I know, I'd mislaid your phone number during the last flat move. Then I bumped into Greg from the course by chance, and he still had your old home number. I'm really sorry; I contacted your ex, as he's still at that number…Soz! But, give him his due, he did pass on your new number to me!"

"Well, it's lovely to hear you…. Where are you now Steph?"

"Latvia."

"Latvia? As in Eastern European Latvia? What the fuck are you doing out there?" I was astounded.

"Riga actually, yeah, I'm teaching English out here."

"When did you become a teacher? You trained as an engineer!" I laughed.

"Two years ago…got made redundant from my last job, another friend had been on a TEFL (Teaching English as a Foreign Language) course at Leeds Metro and gave me a heads-up…I took redundancy and paid for a course, couldn't believe I got offered work overseas so quickly once I gained the qualification. Yeah, was teaching out in Poland first, as soon as I got my Visa!"

I was genuinely shocked. Steph, as I remembered, had a pretty thick Mancunian accent.

Her job had originally been arranged through the British Council, but once over there, she'd seen a better opportunity with a private language school in Warsaw, the Polish Capital. One thing had led to another, connections made, and she'd been offered a contract with another language school out in Riga.

I was curious, why had she got in touch?

Steph explained that she was struggling to keep up with the demand to learn English and was looking to expand her team of tutors. She was now in charge of expansion plans for the school. By chance, she'd been in touch with a mutual contact who'd let her know I was now single.

After a few minutes catching up with our lives, she just blurted out the real reason for the call. "So, do you think you'd like a job teaching overseas?"

I was gobsmacked.

"Steph? Don't be daft; I've got a well-paid job, a lovely little rented house in a great Yorkshire village, and my daughter, hello? Er...No, sorry, not for me luv!" I snorted.

Steph laughed a big belly laugh and cleared the air. We slowly wound up the chat with friendly banter. She eventually had to close as the line started to break up, but she was still pitching to the last,

"Seriously though, if you change your mind, take down my details, get in touch, honestly I think you'd be great at it; I think you've got the real-world skills my students need...you could do this talking job standing on your head!" she laughed.

She signed off with her pithy Mancunian "Byeee Luvv", and I had to smirk to myself at her foreign students picking up her northern intonation. It wasn't exactly Received Pronunciation.

After that nostalgic blast from the past, I quietly carried on with my auto-pilot life for a couple more months. However, something had started to change inside me. Curiosity. This left-field conversation kept going around my head. The timing of this conversation was to be serendipitous.

In hindsight, I could almost believe it was the Universe giving me a signpost direction to a new life. I just had to 'see' it for myself to take action. Like most of us though, we're not brave enough to break free from the status quo; it usually involves a catalyst for change. My opportunity presented itself a few weeks later.

I had been working as an Operational Manager for a large Recruitment firm in Heckmondwike, West Yorks, since my divorce.

It was the flagship office of a group of companies across England. The pay and bonuses were great, but I earned every penny. It was stressful, I had some difficult staffing issues to deal with, and the hours were punishing. My life revolved around the clock. I had to drop my daughter off at nursery on the edge of our village and drive miles to work. The pick-up used to be even more demanding when a new Regional Manager was posted to the same firm.

She was one of the most aggressive, objectionable characters it had been my misfortune to have worked with. Within days, our ego's clashed, and my stress levels rocketed.

This heavily made-up, plump barbie-dollesque would totter up and down the office, interrupt my staff, leaving in her wake enough Chanel perfume to make most cats and dogs in the district follow her home.

My temper started to rise when she began to undermine my authority with my staff and meddle with operational issues. I felt it was a lack of respect. Eventually, the inevitable show-down happened, and I faced her down after a heated meeting. I spoke to my Director about the incident, who seemed to brush off my concerns blithely by saying, "I knew you two Alpha-types would cat-fight!"

"So, you knew about changing my office around and getting my staff to do things without my permission then?" I retorted. My heckles were rising rapidly. A pregnant pause…

"Well, she did…er…mention something…yesterday, I think." She stuttered uncomfortably.

'Fine!' I said.

Now we all know that if someone says fine, it absolutely isn't!

I made up my mind right there and then, I was going to have to change direction, and Steph's phone call rang loudly in my head.

That evening after work, I started to do my research on TEFL teaching courses. The internet was pretty basic compared to today, but I eventually found the course that Steph had mentioned and telephoned for a prospectus.

I couldn't wait for it to be posted. I felt I just had to grit my teeth and try and keep my head down at work for a little longer so that I could leave under MY terms and not get fired or pushed out.

I killed that woman with obsequiousness. She constantly ground my gears; it hadn't gone unnoticed with my staff either, but bless them, they were loyal. They always mentioned to her how great a relationship I had with some of our regular clients. She really couldn't justify getting rid of me. She also knew, because I never missed an opportunity to hint, that I'd take business away from the firm, that I'd make a scene, word would get out in the town, and she'd lose a substantial part of the business.

I wanted to control my exit. The opportunity came very quickly, but I had to prepare the ground carefully. None of my future plans would work without the help of my parents, so I had to do my planning and research carefully.

The TEFL prospectus came, and I immediately telephoned the administrator for further details. I started the ball rolling by gathering all my documentation, proof of my degree and qualifications. I even managed to slip out of the office for an extended lunch break, to nip over to Leeds for an interview with one of the course tutors and view the campus.

I came away with such a tingling fizz of excitement, like I'd been plugged into a current of electricity. I hadn't experienced that feeling for years!

Steph was right, I thought; I love talking, communicating, explaining. It was a comfortable stretch of my skill set. I could do this!

The following weekend, I invited myself down to my parents' for a Sunday lunch. It was a couple of hours away, so not something I did very regularly. They were, of course, delighted to see the 'apple-of-their-eye' Granddaughter.

Both parents busied themselves preparing a proper lunch with homemade Yorkshire puddings and the best flavoured gravy. They put on a good roast. The food was delicious. My girl was spoilt rotten with love and attention.

Mid-way through dessert, whilst the mood was mellow and relaxed, I casually mentioned I was thinking of chucking in my job, studying for a TEFL and working overseas.

There was silence. There were glances exchanged. My dad was mid-forkful, and my mum dropped her spoon. Still silence.

My mum then got up out of her chair, walked up to me, put her hand on mine and said, "Think you're having a mid-life crisis, duck!"

I suddenly burst into tears, my bubble seemed to explode over my head, and a torrent, almost a wail, came out of me. The floodgates of loneliness, unhappiness, stress, anxiety, and trying to keep up the pretence of managing by myself just broke.

"Yes! I probably am! But how would you know Mum? … You've always had Dad to support you, you've never had to struggle out there…On your own (sob)…it's so hard…I'm so unhappy! (wail)".

Dad suddenly ushered my daughter out of the room; she'd looked panicked, darting looks to me, then her Nan, and back to me.

'Mummy, are you alright, Mummy?'

'Mummy's just a bit tired darling…Off you go with Granddad. You go off to the swings, Mum will be okay…Go on.' My mother ushered her out to grab a coat, then came up to me and gave me the longest hug I could ever remember of my adult life.

By suppertime, equilibrium had been restored, and to my total surprise, both Mum and Dad sat me down and announced that they knew I was struggling and unhappy and would give me a break for six months. I'd leave my precious daughter in their charge for a bit; on the proviso I got things organised for her to come over to Warsaw eventually.

I was literally staggered, I felt a flood of relief and hope, but ultimately, I had to gauge my daughter's reaction.

"Darling, what do you think? Would you like to spend some time with Nanny and Granddad whilst Mummy sorts out things for us? Of course you can visit me after a few weeks and Mummy will chat every day and write to you all the time. Hmmm?"

I held my breath. I couldn't have entertained any other option. I really loved my daughter so much, but it wouldn't have been right to traipse her to an unknown situation to begin with. I had to be financially and emotionally stable before she could join me.

"Do you mean stay here now?" She was confused.

"Oh no, not just yet; Mummy's got to sort things out, but next term possibly."

"You mean stay with Nanny and Granddad ALL the time?"

"Yes darling…but not forever, okay?"

I don't think my daughter or I really understood the impact not having each other around for a few months would have. We were, at that moment, excited for different reasons.

We could talk of nothing else on the way home, and though tired when we got in, I had to stop her from pulling out her little weekend case and filling it with cuddly toys to take to her Nanny's. Once settled down for bed, I crept downstairs and took out my big planner and pen.

Anyone who really knows me, understands I'm a list-maker. I love a list. So much so that my lovely girl, when she was older, would make fun of me and write sarcastic little messages at the end of my lists! However, that evening's list was headed:

Immediate Actions & Consequences

I knew as soon as I handed in my notice to quit the company that I'd be given immediate Garden Leave and pretty much escorted off the premises, as they wouldn't want to run the risk of me garnering any client data and causing a fuss.

I had a rainy-day savings fund and figured that with my final salary, I could make it work. Paying for the course, living expenses, and rent until I found a position. It was a risk, but I felt I had to take it.

The following day, I contacted the TEFL Course Administrator and paid for the course. I'd decided to do it full-time and focus on getting it done as quickly as possible. Once I'd paid the fee, I sat down and wrote my resignation letter.

The look on my Regional Manager's face was priceless when I handed it to her.

Headless chickens sprang to mind. A flurry of whispered phone calls to Head Office. A personal plea from my director. By lunchtime, I was off the premises and making arrangements for my company car to be collected. I had access to good public transport, and the train to Leeds was efficient and relatively cheap for the daily commute for classes.

Handing the keys into the Regional Manager's hand, she said something that struck me.

"That sounds really exciting going off to Europe; I wish I was that brave." For a split second, I felt she genuinely meant it. Then, true to form, she couldn't resist a little dig. "Of course, you'll never earn this salary teaching over there, will you?"

I didn't take the bait. I suddenly felt five skins lighter, and the perpetual knot in my stomach eased away. A weird elation. I just grinned and said, "I'm having a mid-life adventure, at last! We'll see, won't we? See ya!"

I hated giving up my big company car, the comfort and status of it. However, as I walked through the exit out into the cool autumn air, I breathed the sweetness of freedom, I started to get my swag on and did something I've never done before or since. As the Regional Manager looked out of her office window, I gave her the finger!

It felt great. I didn't give a shit at that point. I was liberated. She'd made my life so much more difficult than it needed to be at an already stressful time in my life.

But I thank her every day, because she showed me how not to treat people, how not to behave in positions of authority and most importantly, how not to treat a fellow sister.

CHAPTER 2

Homework

The following three months passed by so quickly. My girl and I would set off together in the mornings with pack-ups and stationery in little carry-cases. A friend whose son went to the same Nursery would pick her up (I gave her a contribution to the fuel every week). I would pick her up myself later in the afternoon, and we would return home together on the bus.

The only time I really missed a car was when the weather was foul, with lashing rain and howling winds. Then I'd wistfully imagine sliding into heated leather seats and warm air-con.

The extra walking was good for my figure though, and I started to burn off all the flab and excess booze carbs. Physically, I was getting back into shape.

The course in Leeds was fast-paced and fun. It gave the teaching methods and knowledge needed to plan and deliver lessons and strategies for classroom management. We had to learn to design fun activities, word games to help students learn and absorb vocabulary and grammar. Although for adult learners, they had to be modified.

The British Council is the UK's International organisation for cultural relations and educational opportunities. To gain a position through the British Council (Steph's recommendation), you had to gain a full-time, high-level CELTA (University of Cambridge Certificate in English Language Teaching To Adults). This is the most widely known qualification in the English Language Teaching (ELT) profession.

The classes were small, teaching no more than ten to twelve at a time. So, we got to know our colleagues pretty rapidly. I was a little older than the average student, and because I was a mother, I didn't join in much with the after-school socials. However, they were a friendly rag-tag bunch of young people freshly qualified from University and wanting the opportunity to work and travel around the world using their teaching skills to fund their travels. Quite a few were more mature and were seeking a change of pace from corporate burn-out or being made redundant and looking for fresh challenges.

CELTA is a popular qualification as there is no final exam. Evaluation is all practical. There is an observed final lesson where you're marked and graded on your ability to plan, deliver and execute a lesson, despite staged real-world distractions.

The ability to think on your feet is a big skill, and the ability to use non-verbal communication and tone of voice, a bit like when you puppy train a dog, is also helpful!

One of the best parts of the course was guidance on how to find work Overseas as an English Teacher. Demand grows every year from abroad to learn English so that countries can engage in a global economy. Having a CELTA opens doors to the most prestigious language schools around the World.

I loved my homework. I'd regularly stay up late into the night, diligently working through my assignments. This wasn't a cheap course, and I'd thrown up my job to do it. I was seriously committed!

Isn't it strange though, that when you work hard on activities that excite you, time seems to evaporate? When you toil away on something that gives you no joy, time stretches out and drags.

I was busy and productive, ironically spending more time with my daughter. Focused and enjoying new challenges, but I was already burning through my savings at an alarming rate, more than I'd initially budgeted for.

I didn't want a state handout, so I made a radical decision. I decided to give up my rented home in West Yorks, temporarily return to living with my parents in Peterborough as soon as I had qualified, and hope I'd get a position Overseas as quickly as Steph had suggested.

It meant more upheaval for us. Children are resilient, but it doesn't mean there's not a price to pay somewhere down the tracks. Years later, the constant uprooting, living abroad, finding new schools, making new sets of friends, and learning new cultures took its toll on her mental state. Her anxiety levels ramped up, and she became a hoarder.

Her teenage room was an epic refuge for the tat and ephemera that teenage girls can collect. It was beyond messy and chaotic, despite my nagging, which was ignored. By the time she left home to go to University in Sheffield, I'd suspected it had something to do with building a little sanctuary around her that she could control. An unconscious clutter-castle for protection from life's vagaries and upheavals.

As an adult, she's dealing with some of those demons now, but I had a great deal of guilt about what I put her through in the process of finding myself again. Every now and again, she'll have too much to drink and cruelly let me know, in no uncertain terms, how she hated being uprooted.

I believe she gained more than she lost during this period of our lives. She got to spend quality time with both my parents, who adored her. This created a strong, lasting bond. She adapted fast and became very articulate and mature for her age as she adopted self-sufficiency, and a sense of humour as coping strategies to be quickly liked and accepted wherever she ended up.

After breezing through my studies, I packed up and returned to my parents' home with my daughter late in 1998. It was Advent-time, so excitement was building up to Christmas, and I managed to find temporary work to help swell my dwindling coffers.

Whilst I'll always be so grateful to both my parents at the time for allowing us back home and giving us a roof over our heads with love and support, no adult child really enjoys returning home to their family home with their parents.

"What time will you be home, duck?"

"Do you want your dinner saving?"

"Don't you think you've had enough to drink?"

"Why have you bought that?"

A hundred explanations a day, although not unkind, just made me feel infantilised.

The worst though, was the slight undermining of my authority with my child. She would sometimes exploit this situation ruthlessly, as let's be honest, children do, and had amassed a growing collection of teddies, cuddly toys and plastic objects only a six-year-old could covet.

My parents had lived in my family home all their married life up to this date. I was raised there, and returning to my own room, minus the Donny Osmond posters, seemed weirdly familiar yet odd. The local Junior school I had attended was going to be my daughter's new school - Fulbridge Road Juniors.

As soon as I stepped into that school, the memories came hurtling back to greet me like a long-forgotten friend. I had been a happy child there.

I'd enjoyed learning in that old-fashioned, well-preserved nineteenth-century building with impossibly high glass windows. I loved being Window Monitor. This involved collecting a large pole with a brass hook arrangement on the end of it. Once I'd mastered the technique of hooking the hook through the overpainted metal ring shape on the frame of the lower window lights, it would create a noisy creak and clang as it created the necessary ventilation.

I would always take the opportunity to stare out of the windows and nosey at the world outside the school gates that carried on regardless.

The smell was instantly recognisable. A combination of beeswax and bleach. There was another jogging of the memory too. One of my class teachers had now become the Headmaster. I was amazed to find his name in the school prospectus. Like all children, we assume adults are so old. I had expected him to have expired years ago. It was a shock to find out he was only nearly sixty, which by my computation, would have made him late twenties when he taught me.

Mr Smythe used to put the fear of God into me as a child. He was a tall Yorkshireman, ramrod straight. A very square jaw, like a piece of Yorkshire granite and a shock of still yellow blonde hair. Looking like a weathered Viking, he had the deepest, most piercing blue eyes that could detect wrongdoing at fifty paces!

He had tremendous 'presence'. I sat up straighter when he entered his office. He was firm but very fair and a very kind soul. Seeing him again after thirty years made me a little flustered when he suddenly stooped down, head cocked, boring those blue eyes into me, and asked,

"Are you Lesley Williams?"

"Good grief!" I exclaimed. "How did you recognise me? It's thirty years ago?"

"The address, same address, then the eyes; obviously, other stuff has changed' he said, waving his hand in front of me. 'Even the colour of y'hair and that." He grinned.

"Now then! This young 'un is the mark two version, is she? What's tha'name, young miss?" He smiled.

My daughter started to wrap herself around my legs for protection as she said shyly, "I'm Rebecca…We've moved from Yorkshire, you know."

"Well, good, you'll know it's God's own county then!" He laughed.

"…and we won the War of the Roses…" She carried on.

"Clever lass aren't you, eh? …Well remembered lass."

Before he could launch into a mini-lesson, I cut in, to ask about enrolment procedures.

Of course, my daughter couldn't wait to get back to her Nan's and tell her she had the same teacher as her Mummy and that he was from "God's own county, you know Nan, the one that won the War of the Roses!"

CHAPTER 3

Saying Goodbye

January is a rotten time I think in terms of the British weather. It starts to get seriously grim, filthy and grey. My general mood plummets and my emotions are affected by the poor light at this time of the year. I wasn't diagnosed as such back then, but later as S.A.D. (Seasonal Affective Disorder syndrome). It feels like from Christmas onwards that someone has smothered me with a slate duvet cover. I feel a heaviness and unexplainable melancholy.

After the festivities, I was very flat. My temporary work had dried up after the sales. Whilst I'd topped up my savings, I'd not heard back from the Careers Service Department at Leeds Metropolitan about my Tutor interview and Language School recommendations. I was in limbo.

I had, nonetheless, started to prepare for my departure overseas, and although she was an incredibly bright and intuitive child, my daughter was still only six. She was a tad too young to fully understand that Mummy would be away for at least six months, that, give or take a couple of visits, I wouldn't be around physically every day.

I tried to make the planning and preparation seem exciting and did involve her. We talked about Poland and the culture and some foods. We had a big Atlas, and my Dad would talk to her and weave in stories about his National Service and the interesting countries he'd visited in the Army.

I started to collect little keepsakes for her. I found a funky, brightly coloured mug that had the logo 'Top Girl' on it. She cherished that mug for many years. Indeed, it came to a crashing end when she was in her twenties, in a house move from London. It wasn't like it was Dresden china, it was of ordinary manufacture, but it was priceless to her as something her Mummy had hand-picked out especially to remind her that she was loved.

I'll never fully know how I could have left my beautiful little girl. Just remembering her crumpled angelic face at the mere mention of me leaving England brings the tears back to my eyes.

Finally, in mid-January, a letter arrived from the British Council. I tore it open, then held my breath as I scanned the contents.

Relief flooded through me; I'd done it- passed everything, Observations, Tutor interview, the lot!

I read further; in addition, due to my work and life experiences, a well-respected Language Study Centre had expressed an interest and had offered a six-month contract to teach Business English to adults in Warsaw.

I was to contact them directly to confirm details and to prepare to take up post by mid-February 1999.

I held the letter in my hand for a long time. This was the opportunity I'd been praying for, a fresh start, an adventure. Then the realisation hit that the cost of doing this would be the real separation from my daughter if I was to make it work.

I was elated and yet panicked at the same time. This was becoming a reality, not a pipe-dream or a brag to friends about having a mid-life crisis experience and travel opportunities.

I was going to Poland. I was going to teach highly educated Polish executives the nuances of my mother tongue. I was going to be paid in dollars, hard currency. Before Poland joined the Euro, dollars had real spending power with a better exchange rate. My meagre teaching salary would effectively be at least twice the average worker's income, meaning I could live quite comfortably.

The gamble had paid off so far, and just in the nick of time to boost my blue mood.

My mind was buzzing with the inevitable 'To Do' lists that were rapidly growing in my head. The first tick off the list was to book my travel tickets to Warsaw. One of the funniest exchanges happened when I went to book my intercontinental coach tickets. I loathe flying. I don't enjoy it one little bit and will always find alternatives first, only doing it if I absolutely have to.

I was quite prepared to swap out the three-hour hell of flying for a thirty-six-hour coach ride; it was a heck of a lot cheaper, and it wasn't flying! However, purchasing the tickets over the phone with National Coaches became something of a comedy sketch.

"Hello, I'm looking to travel to Warsaw. I've got to be in Warsaw by February 18th. Could you advise me on prices and the itinerary, please?"

"Okay chick." (She was a Brummie.) "Well, the coach leaves London Victoria Coach Station at 0600hrs and arrives at Walsall Station, 0845hrs 18th Feb…. that'll be £18 please."

"No, sorry, Warsaw."

"That's it…Walsall, yes?"

"No! Warsaw…You know, Capital of Poland?" I shouted.

"Warsaw, not Walsall…oh…W-a-r-s-a-w! Oh, I'm a silly wench! Thought it was up the road in Walsall, West Mids!" She giggled. "Oh…righto…that's very different, then, just give me a minute to work this lot out…there's places here, I've never 'eard of 'em! Can I call yer back, chick?"

It seemed to take forever, but eventually she returned my call.

"Hello, so you wanted to go by coach all the way to Poland? So, working back from February 18th, I've got a couple of options for you chick, but both of them will involve a stop-over at a German Tourist hotel. You alright with that?"

"What's that for?"

"Oh, it's the border thing…you know, German Border Control." This was in the days before Poland had joined the EU.

"Okay, don't really have an option, do I?"

"No, chick ya don't."

Starting off from London, Victoria Coach Station, she rattled off all the pick-up points to the Channel Port at Dover, the ferry timings, and then various towns and cities en route into the Low Countries until we met the German border.

A stopover in a small tourist B&B to freshen up and have a meal, before a couple of stops in Poland to the Capital.

I scribbled down all the information. I felt like Jules Verne! It most definitely sounded like an adventure!

As I started to tick off items on my 'to-do' list and had a firm start date, I now had to start thinking about packing a case that would cover all my clothing needs in the early days.

I knew from the correspondence with the Language School that they'd given me a survival list of clothes and personal effects to bring over. However, it seemed pretty short. Two jumpers, it's freezingly cold in Poland during the winter months, one pair of jeans and so on.

The list just didn't cut it with me. Don't get me wrong, I'm no fashionista, but I had visions of schlepping around in grungy student wear, which was not my style at all. Not to mention the professional offices I'd be sent to teach in. No stipulation of smart business attire at all.

Obviously, I'd overlooked the fact that Warsaw had shops! For some reason, I had imagined the shops were a bit bare and post-Soviet drab. How wrong I was. The Secretaries at the school gave me a link to a few decent department stores in the central shopping district of the Nowy Swiat (New Street). It looked like the Champs D'Elyse in Paris!

Smart, glossy, and relatively expensive designer brand shop fronts that wouldn't look out of place in London or Milan. They suggested bringing the bare minimum as I'd have less to lug around, then hit the shops once settled for a decent business suit.

Warsaw would continue to blow my fairly low expectations out of the water from day one if I was honest.

Poland was developing rapidly at this time. It was looking to become the financial beating heart of Eastern Europe. So many corporations had set up their head offices in the capital.

International Banks and blue-chip brands like Volvo, Coca-Cola, and MGM, to name but a few. Educated Poles had a new Western viewpoint, no longer shackled to their Soviet oppressors in Russia. The country was looking to re-train for a service economy and teach English as a second business language in their schools. No one wanted to discuss Russian politics or language.

Language Schools were springing up like mushrooms. I wouldn't be out of work even if I freelanced. I had an in-demand skill as a native-English speaker, and everyone, I mean everyone, wanted to learn English. It was boom time.

I felt I owed Steph a call to explain, to thank her very much for the inspiration, but that I would be going out to Poland (like she had done initially) instead of setting up in Riga.

I felt that Warsaw was more 'Western' in its outlook than Riga, which had a very large Russian population and culturally, I didn't think it was as developed as Poland.

She was incredibly generous and said if it didn't quite work out, she'd give me a job in a heartbeat. She really was a good friend, and it gave me confidence that I was on the right pathway to new opportunities.

I'd done everything I could have done to prepare for this adventure. Obtaining the Visa had entailed a long trip down to London and back in one day, but it had been a breeze. Just paperwork and rubber stamps. I had an official job offer from the Language School that was verified with a quick phone call to confirm, then plonk! The eagle crest of the Polish flag was thumped across my passport pages in bright green ink. I had six months before I had to get it re-stamped or go home. The countdown to my fateful separation from my daughter had begun.

She had started to get clingy the week before my departure; she knew change was in the air. She had settled into her new school really well and had made some new friends my Mum and I encouraged her to bring home for teatime visits. I wanted her to feel like this was a positive change, but she was still very young and just wanted hugging more.

The night before my departure, I'd slept next to her in my bed. Watching her eventually drop off to sleep reminded me of the time after giving birth; I'd just sat up and marvelled at her perfectly lovely little face in complete wonderment and pure mother-love.

My little angel, I turned over and quietly sobbed into my pillow. I very nearly called the whole endeavour off. Why did I always seem to make my life so complicated?

Ideally, I would have taken her with me as my little travelling companion, but sensibly, my parents were right to insist she stay with them for a while.

It could have been a nightmare travelling alone with a six-year-old. An upended routine, uncomfortable travel with strangers, and weird and exotic food to manage. No, it was the right decision, but my heart was broken.

I'd resolved to communicate with her EVERY day somehow, either by telephone or, more often, with a Bluey.

Anyone who had ever been in the Forces or had had a 'pen-pal' overseas years ago would understand the term Bluey. It was the feather-light, blue and red chevron-edged stationery. In the days of 'snail-mail', there was a certain excitement in waiting for the Bluey to arrive.

It commanded respect because it had travelled far. Don't forget; these were the days before iPhones, apps and great internet coverage. My parents didn't even have a computer at home.

I had an alarm set for 6 am; the taxi to take me to Peterborough Coach Station was coming at 7 am. My daughter stirred a little, but I silently let her slumber whilst I quickly freshened up and put the last of the toiletries in my already prepared hand luggage, sat next to my large, sturdy case propped up like a billboard in the hallway. When she'd got ready for bed, she had noticed it like a red sign of departure. Her bottom lip had trembled, and she'd wanted carrying up to her bed. She knew that by the morning her little world would be changing.

Dad had asked if I'd wanted a bacon sandwich for breakfast. I felt queasy and churned up with apprehension. So, my parents and I sat in the dining kitchen, drinking tea in utter silence. Clearly nervous about the impending sad farewell that was coming up, my Dad paced up and down the hallway, looking out for the taxi lights.

When the taxi arrived on the dot, it quietly flashed its lights. Dad opened the door to take out the cases, and I raced upstairs to scoop up my precious child. Mum and Dad came up the stairs, and we all embraced on the stairs landing.

I smothered my child's little face with kisses, wet from the inevitable tears streaming down my face. Still bleary-eyed, she flung her little arms around my neck so tight it was almost painful. Then Dad took over, and I transferred her into his arms as she started to really cry her little heart out. Her Nan gave her a favourite cuddly toy.

We all embraced for the final time; my parents told me they loved me and to contact them as soon as I could on the ferry so they wouldn't worry, and to keep me posted about the journey.

They were all downstairs standing out on the porch, backlit with the hall light, when I made the mistake of looking back as the taxi pulled away. My child was being cradled by Mum and Dad, and I could see my Mum's worried face cast down towards Dad's chest, where wailing, my daughter had buried her little head.

"Mummy....Muuummmyyyy, come back Mummmmmmy."

I put my hand on the glass as a final gesture, then put my hand over my mouth to stop the sound of a huge sob from escaping.

The Taxi driver was probably experienced in witnessing goodbyes, so he tactfully never said a word until I was dropped off ten minutes later. I'd barely composed myself when looking for the coach bay to London, where I was joined by others.

This was it. The start. No going back now.

I trundled my case out to the awaiting National Coach with others in a colourful crocodile of leisurewear, trainers, and backpacks. I handed over my tickets; it was matched with the itinerary, my case was stowed, and I went to find a window seat.

The Steward was already brewing tea and coffee and handing it out. I gratefully drank it down to clear my throat and then felt incredibly hungry. I remembered my snack pack in my hand luggage and wolfed down an apple and a chocolate bar.

I felt like the worst mother in the world and a runaway to boot. There were more silent sobs, more dabbing eyes as we revved up and started the long boring haul down to London.

It was a misty, gloomy, cold and grey February morning. There was a soft drizzle, and the incessant scratching of perished window wipers just added to the depressing soundscape.

I tried to rest. I think I nodded off just past St. Neots. I honestly don't remember the rest of the trip until about fifteen minutes before we pulled into Victoria Coach Station.

Another coffee to revive once in the concourse. Much milling about and killing time eating a bacon sandwich waiting for the connection. Final calls to International destinations, then finally on to Warsaw.

Passports checked. luggage secured. Coach driver introductions in English and Polish. There were many returning Poles on board, whole families, excitedly jabbering in Polish as we set off.

I had my trusty cassette recorder, earphones, a good thick reading book, a pocket phrasebook, and a brand-new brick-like mobile phone. This phone was my umbilicus to my daughter and my life back in the UK. I was as prepared as I was going to be to begin this journey, this odyssey of rediscovering my creativity and joy.

I was ready for whatever life was out there for me to find!

CHAPTER 4

Coach Traveller

I'm a great believer in being brave and trying out new things and experiences. However, I'll be perfectly honest, travelling thirty-six hours in a sweaty, intercontinental coach with a backed-up on-board toilet, hearing the constant wail of fractious babies, toddlers and Europop constantly blaring on the radio, is not an experience to be repeated!

After an uneventful ferry crossing, I could have written reams about all the cool sights through the Low Countries and interesting urban European towns and cities. How fascinating the passengers were as we swapped life stories to fill the hours. I could, but it would be a figment of my imagination. The honest truth is, it was all so grim that I think I've blocked some of it from my memory.

Sitting in cramped and uncomfortable coach seats aggrivated my sciatica down one leg. I was constantly fidgeting, trying to alleviate the stabbing pain.

I was also bored out of my gourd listing to the same 20-song playlist I had carefully curated on an old-fashioned tape cassette. 'Ells Travel Songs', after the twentieth play, got on my wick. So much so I actually started to listen to the Europop songs and developed a liking for cheesy-Eurovision dance music!

I'd finished reading a large autobiography, the size of a good doorstep, by Alan Bennet within the first six hours. I didn't know enough Polish to undertake even a basic conversation, so I basically slept for as long as I could.

The most excitement was the stop-over at a small tourist B&B, where we all had to troop off to segregated dormitory-style rooms, men one side of the corridor, women on the other. We were all so tired, but also hungry, so many of us ate the 'plat du jour', a hearty, tasty stew. Vegans were not catered for at this time. It simply wasn't an option!

There was some fairly basic, rough red wine on offer, which I swilled down, then went to the rudimentary shower-block to freshen up. Before I turned in for the night, I was offered a shot of vodka by an elderly couple. I didn't like to refuse their kind hospitality, so I knocked it back. It was the perfect nightcap. I barely remember a thing after that; I must have fallen asleep in seconds.

I was rudely awoken in the morning with a start. Dogs were barking frantically, then a revving coach engine. Gawd! They wouldn't leave without me? I thought in a panic. No, but the coach was crawling with uniformed German Border Guards with machine guns. We were literally at the German Border. I hadn't grasped how close we were to the frontier.

No mucking about; these guards were using sniffer dogs to check for drug smuggling. Everyone was questioned, had our passports scrutinised, and our luggage checked. It's unbelievable now with open European borders, but back in the 1990s, Poland hadn't joined the EU.

This bureaucracy took ages. I mean hours and hours. We were all so bored of hanging around, children became fractious, and tempers started to rise. I vowed never to spend so long on a coach again. It cured my fear of flying. However, many Polish people regularly made this very trip. I resolved to stop moaning to myself and add it to my mental file entitled, 'Life's Rich Tapestry'.

Eventually, we were waved quickly onboard; the driver babbled something in Polish (I'm guessing it was something very rude about German guards) as the bus erupted with snorting laughter and nodding looks across the aisles as we roared off to continue the final stages of the trip.

The mood lifted, the radio started playing some popular Polish songs, and the coach almost had a carnival atmosphere as we entered Polish territory. Some were longing to return home and could sense it wouldn't be so long now.

Northern Poland is a very flat country. A bit like the Fens region of East Anglia. Endless plains, with very little to alleviate the eye line. No wonder Poland had been invaded by Russia and Germany over the years in major wars. Nothing really to hold up tanks over that flat topography. Miles and miles of drab homesteads, tatty towns, peasants working in fields, wrapped up in many warm layers against the bitterly cold conditions.

There then began a shift in energy and rising excitement onboard the coach. Much shuffling of bags and standing up to gather belongings from overhead storage. More chatter, and then, just as twilight fell, we could start to see the bright lights of Warsovian suburbs. A little later, the illuminated Palace of Culture & Science could be seen.

The Palace is in the very centre of Warsaw. It was a 'gift' from Stalin and was nicknamed 'The Wedding Cake' because of its tiered appearance.

During Soviet times, it was bristling with surveillance equipment from the Kremlin and was a detested symbol of Russian oppression to the Poles. Due to the very flat skyline, 'Big-Brother' Russia was always watching, listening, and checking up on their Polish neighbours.

When I first went to Poland, you could see this building from all over the city. Today, it is different. It has been ringed with confident and amazing post-modern skyscrapers and dramatic architectural wonders to distract the eye away from its prominence.

However, on my arrival into Warsaw, it did look striking in the haze of an early winter evening as it was lit up like it had a thousand candles inside. My heart started to pound, and my adrenaline rose. Where was my phrase book? I would need that to survive. Making sure I had everything to hand, I waited for the coach to finally alight at Warsaw Coach Station.

Finally having everything checked off, clutching tickets, and retrieving my large case, I trundled off to the slightly care-worn coach station. First impressions were tempered by the bone-chilling cold. I had sensibly put on several layers after my dad had given me a tip: lots of thin layers, not big, thick woolly jumpers. The secret was in allowing the air trapped around the body and between the layers to "insulate" you from the worst of the cold. Plus, it meant I didn't need to stuff so many thick woollens into my case!

Even so, my first impression of a Polish winter was that my breath was freezing onto the scarf that I had wrapped around my mouth and neck. White frosted beads formed tiny icicles across my mouth, and it was unpleasant to breathe. I didn't realise it at the time, but it was about -18 degrees Centigrade and forecasted to snow overnight.

I stopped to scrabble about in my hand luggage for another couple of thin layers to bulk out my thick, long grey cashmere coat. I plonked on a mismatched woolly hat, pulled my scarf over my nose, and made my way like an intrepid Arctic explorer to the concourse.

I felt a mixture of blind panic, bewilderment, relief, and yawning tiredness.

I just wanted to rendezvous with the Language School Representative with whom I'd had contact back in the UK. He promised to meet me here at the allotted time and guide me to the hotel, which was going to be my temporary home for the next month.

This was all part of my employment contract. I had to pay for the hotel myself, but they would do everything else to support my settling in and help to find more permanent accommodation in the city.

As I waited for my contact to appear, I realised I had about fifteen minutes to kill. I felt exposed and vulnerable, a real fish out of water. I was struggling to gain my bearings and was also incredibly thirsty. I'd not drunk too much that day because the toilet on the coach was overflowing. The stench was disgusting, and I just didn't want to spend my first hour in Warsaw hunting down a toilet!

I noticed a small kiosk in the central concourse with a bright green illuminated sign, 'Herbata'. It was a tea and snack kiosk. Tea. The great reviver. Just what I needed to steady my nerves and warm me up. I had a quick check of my trusty phrasebook; yes, herbata was definitely Polish for tea. I screwed up my courage and reticence and blurted out, "Herbata proposze" and pointed at the steaming tea-urn.

The dumpy, over-made-up woman serving me smiled and quickly made a steaming cup of weak black tea (they don't tend to serve it with milk). I handed over a note in local currency and was given a pile of coins in return; I had no idea if I'd been overcharged and she'd made a tidy profit out of me. (I later found out she had, the tea had cost me £2.50, which at the time in Poland was very expensive!)

It didn't matter. I was so grateful and felt immediately comforted and elated. Firstly, I could make myself understood, and secondly, the heat from the scalding hot liquid was seeping through the polystyrene cup holder and warming me up with every sip.

After the last dregs were drunk, I started to feel anxious again.

He was five minutes late. What if he didn't show up? I would be well and truly screwed. Yes, I had an address for the hotel, but honestly, I felt like I had just landed on a new uncharted frozen planet. It was all so alien to me.

Okay, don't panic. I had a phone number…dialling the given contact number, I listened to the weird foreign dialling tone.

Then a click,

"Hello?"

"Oh, Hello! Graham? Sorry…er…This Is Ellie LaCrosse, new teacher…. erm…. I'm at the Coach Station…did we arrange a pick-up for 7 pm?"

"Oh. Hello! …Yes! …(breathless)…er…yes! I'm on my way, just got caught up with things. Tram is rammed, and I've just left the School…sorry, I'll be about another five minutes. You okay there?" He sounded concerned.

Relief flooded through me. He sounded like the cavalry coming to rescue a stranded damsel. "Oh yes…fine, fine…had a cup of tea from the kiosk already…yes, just fine." I sighed. I was going to be safe.

When Graham approached me, I was facing away from him, and when he tapped me on the shoulder, I let out a little squeal.

"Oh, Sorry! Hello, Ellie?" He gabbled and shot his hand out to shake mine. "Let me take that big case for you. Gosh! It's heavy; how the heck did you manage that? I've got a taxi waiting for us…we'll be going straight to the hotel. Let's go." He sounded breezy and efficient.

I trotted off with this almost stranger. When I think back, I was vulnerable and completely trusting of this man. I could have been lured away. But I wasn't. He was wearing a bright blue lanyard with the School logo on, which swung over his oversized brown tweed coat.

With pale blue eyes and a shock of ginger hair and beard, my first impression of him was that he looked like a large, orange, teddy bear.

Graham was, in fact, a senior teacher at the Language School and was going to be my line manager and mentor. He chatted amiably about my trip; in fact, he chattered non-stop from the Bus Station to the Hotel Polonia. The hotel was a grand-looking building on the Aleja Jerozolimskie, a huge thoroughfare cutting across east-west of the city.

He helped me check-in and directed a young hotel porter to haul my cases up to the room. Once in the room, he quickly scanned all around, smiled and said:

"Okay! Well, you're here! Just like to say, we're all looking forward to you joining the native-English-speaking team…I bet you're absolutely knackered, so I'll get out of your hair. I'll give you a day or two to draw breath and find your feet, so I'll call you at 9 am the day after tomorrow to escort you to the language school and start your Induction. It's not that far really, you could walk it from here, but to make sure you don't get lost I'll collect you. Plus, the weather's closing in; snow's forecasted to be really heavy over the next few days…(sigh)…get used to it; it snows a lot in winter. I mean proper snow…not the apprentice stuff back in the UK!" He laughed.

Then he handed me a little booklet of paper strips. "You'll need these; they're tram-tickets; it's a weekly block. Punch a hole in each one on each trip. Do not forget. They are REALLY strict about fare-dodging on trams in Warsaw! Inspectors tend to be ex-military and are scary! Okay. There's enough for the first week. Right, time for me to go." He nodded his head, shook my hand, and ambled out.

I was numb. So much information to digest. I was overwhelmed and bone-tired.

I knew breakfast was hours away, but I was ravenous with hunger. So I fumbled into my backpack, ate the rest of my emergency snack rations, and made a cup of tea., The sugary snack made me sleepy, and my eyes felt like lead. I didn't unpack, wash or change out of my clothes. Instead, I literally flopped onto the bed and pulled the top cover over me. Blithely unaware of anything else, I started to doze off.

Then, as if my maternal instinct alarm went off, I remembered I had to contact home. I'd promised Mum and Dad. I fumbled for my phone, forgetting about the time difference, and a slightly dazed Mum answered.

It was a very perfunctory call; we were both tired. I asked her to let my child know her mummy was safe; she said she had settled down okay after a few little tears. She was glad I'd arrived safely and told me to get some sleep.

Returning to my foetal sleeping position, I immediately fell into a deep, deep slumber.

My 2000-mile trip to escape the familiar but damaged me had concluded, and the real journey of rediscovering Ellie was just about to begin.

CHAPTER 5

Early Days

I have a striking memory of my first day in Warsaw. I was out cold for ten hours straight. I awoke to an alarm on my phone that I'd had the presence of mind to set whilst I tore into my emergency snack ration. I do love my food, and I didn't want to miss breakfast.

As I rolled off the bed, I felt slightly disgusted at myself. I stank of body odour, having not had a proper wash in two days. My hair was plastered across my head, and my travelling clothes were grubby and crumpled. I needed a good wash and scrub up; time to check out the hotel room's facilities.

I wasn't disappointed, I hadn't realised it at the time I'd arrived, but this was a pretty good standard tourist hotel. It was built to accommodate visiting Russian officials back when Poland was part of the USSR.

It had a very grand Lobby area and an over-the-top-ornate, grand central staircase. It reminded me of something Disney would draw for a Princess; I had a little daydream of me floating down in some gorgeous dress.

The lift system had inlaid wooden panels depicting Polish folklore scenes, and worn-brass controls, worn bright by years of punching floor destinations. Every bedroom overlooking the city had a small balcony. I was fortunate to get a front-facing room. The hotel was a little faded, but she had obviously been plush in her Soviet-era heyday.

Hot water gushed from the tap into a deep, enamelled bath. I'd learnt from experience not to trust any shower over the bath system. They always seemed to squirt rain showers of cold water where I didn't want it!

I did my ablutions in quick order, freshened up my hairstyle and put on some light make-up. Then I unpacked a warm, stylish woollen dress, thick tights and boots and hurried off to catch the last of the breakfast.

The dining room was vast. It looked like a cross between a layered wedding cake and the inside of a theatre, with theatre boxes around the upper gallery complete with huge red swags in red velvet.

I later found out it had been a theatre back in the 1950s when the hotel was built.

The smell of something akin to bacon tickled my nostrils, and I made a beeline for the server area along one side of this vast dining room.

Many platters with domes were being lifted and closed by the waiters, looking very smart and clean-cut. They reminded me of athletic penguins, preening, twitching, and trying to orchestrate the smooth running of the breakfast offering along the buffet tables.

Once opened, the silver platters revealed an international menu ranging from toasts made with numerous choices of bread to various white and oily fish and many platters containing different kinds of meat and cheese.

I kept it very simple. A trusty fried egg on toast with a side of Kielbasa sausage. There's something about seeing a buffet table; it always makes me overeat; my brain acts like a kid in a sweet shop. "Ohhh, that looks tasty; I'll try a bit of that; hmmm…I'll have a couple of those pastry things or a croissant or two as well; they look so delicious!"

The waiters kept fussing around me. There must have been at least four in attendance, all coming up and asking if I was happy with the food. Did I need more coffee? More pastry Pana (Miss)?

I really wanted to be left alone to take in the sensory tableaux in front of my eyes. I was basically eating an enormous breakfast inside a theatre. A novel experience.

When I had eaten half my body weight, I retired to my bedroom and caught my breath as it had started to snow.

I just sat and watched snowflakes as big as pebbles flutter and swirl over the grey winter skyline and settle like a huge white duvet. It softened all the hard edges of ugly, drab Stalinist tower block apartments, and it made all the wide freeways look like white spokes spanning out from the Centrum district.

Warsaw is a busy city, but suddenly the constant thrum of traffic grew quieter, muffled. The snow had the effect of dampening down the sound. It really struck me how beautifully spectacular the snow made the city skyline. The crystalline snow glinted like sparkling glass beads thrown underfoot. It was virgin, pristine, and made the city look magical.

I was captivated by the views and fell in love with the City right there and then.

I suddenly felt sleepy again, and I dozed for about twenty minutes until I was snapped out of my reverie by a harsh knocking on my door. It was Housekeeping, wanting to clean my room. It was my cue to get out and explore the city!

I quickly realised that getting dressed for an Eastern European winter was not a simple case of 'throw on some joggies and trainers and out the door!"

It involved a strategic layering up of several thin tops, leggings, socks, jacket/coat, hat, scarf, and gloves. There was definitely an art to it all. I emerged from my hotel room looking like an Inuit, ready for a hunting expedition to the Polar Ice caps. I was already perspiring by the time I had descended into the gleaming lobby.

There were some very glamorous-looking women sitting, chatting, or wafting about in the Lobby looking very 'Anna Karenina', Tolstoy's haughty aristocratic heroine. They all appeared, tall, leggy, and absolutely not wearing a cagoule and a hat with a woolly pompom. I stood out like a sore thumb. I felt and looked like a bag-lady with mismatched layers and roundly comfy appearance. I felt warm but looked a hot mess.

As I stepped outside, for my very first day to explore this unknown city, I was shocked at the bone-chilling air piercing my lungs. It was dry, ice-cold, numbing, and uncomfortable to breathe. I looked around me and realised everyone was breathing through a scarf or covering over their mouth and nose. Ice crystals clung to exposed parts of my face, and wispy smoke-like tendrils rose up and around people's faces.

How was I going to function in this city, which was like this for months on end?

I'd arrived mid-February, towards the tail-end of winter, several weeks away from spring. I had an overwhelming desire to scuttle back to the warmth of the hotel and snuggle under my duvet, but I needed to start to gain my bearings.

Passers-by were wearing hats of all shapes and sizes. There were many jaunty large velvet berets worn by the women, which I thought were very stylish. I'd never seen anything similar in France, and certainly not in the UK. My woolly bobble-hat looked a bit thin and weedy, so I resolved to invest in a proper Warszovian fur hat.

Passing a few hat shops close to the hotel persuaded me to venture to try a few on. Using prosze and the universal pointy-finger language, I finally settled on a beautiful silver and black-tipped fake-fur hat. Instant glamour!

When later, I returned to the hotel, I matched it with my one decent winter cashmere coat that nearly grazed the floor and had a flirty swing with a slightly militaristic look to it; I could blend in and look like a Warszovian woman gracing those cobbled streets in the Old-Town.

Many months later, when my daughter came over to visit, she said,

"Why does your hat look like you have you've got a dead rabbit on your head Mummy?"

Now my head was warm and toasty, I felt emboldened to walk around the snow-covered avenues around my hotel. I didn't want to catch a tram until I'd made a brain-map in my head of the surrounding locale so that I could recognise buildings.

The biggest challenge for me has always been my spatial awareness. For some reason, I have directional issues. My brain always seems to be 180 degrees off my actual route of travel.

I spent my first real day in Warsaw walking, trying to follow a map (no Google maps then) and getting lost!

I must have walked at least five miles before hunger and thirst drove me to try to feed myself. By some miracle, I had arrived in the very centre of the city at the picturesque Old Town Square, Rynek Starego Miasta. The place was bustling with people and tourists and surrounded by restaurants and cafes.

I saw delicious, displayed cakes and breads in an attractive looking bakery, piekarnia; I went inside and pointed to a cheesecake, Sernik. It was sliced up and bagged very elaborately. I ate it sat on a bench around the edge of the square and drank some hot chocolate from the same piekarnia.

I felt like I'd burnt off all the breakfast calories walking for miles and could manage more carbs!

As I sat and drank the most delicious liquid hot chocolate, I felt strangely comforted that I could eat and drink and not starve in this foreign city.

I relaxed about my decision to upend my life and traipse several thousands of miles to a slightly unknown part of the world. As I mentioned earlier, I was oddly fascinated by the history of

WWII. From day one, entering this rebuilt city of Warsaw, you could not escape the city's trauma and past war scars.

I'd counted several brass plaques on many street corners as I roamed around the districts. They all gleamed bright and either had flowers, candles, or both, freshly displayed. They were obviously regularly tended. The wording was very direct.

No-one is really allowed to forget the huge sacrifices made by the Polish population, especially the Polish Jewish population in the city.

It was a daily, poignant reminder that Warsaw was rebuilt after being razed to the ground in 1945. To a certain extent, by the late 1990s and early 2000s, Warsaw's faux-rebuilt medieval Old Town had acquired a patina of age and didn't look Disney-fake.

However, a brief look across the River Vistula to the drab Stalinist apartment blocks built in the regeneration and rebuilding of the city in the 1950s and 60s gave an indication of the scale of the destruction this city suffered. It was endless grey, plain and somehow sullen.

I spent the rest of the day ambling about the very centre of the city, just absorbing snippets of Polish, sliding about on slushy pavements and realising I had better learn some survival Polish pretty quickly.

'Please' prosze and 'Thank you' dzienkuje, I had already mastered. I spent the rest of the day learning and using 'please speak more slowly' Prose mowic wolneij, and 'I don't understand', Nie rozumien!

By the time I'd returned to the Hotel Polonia, it was late afternoon, and I was footsore. Grateful that, in my mind, it was now my 'home' for the next few weeks. As I entered through the revolving door into the plush lobby, the Concierge nodded to me. He had already clocked that I was English. (I think the bobble hat initially gave it away!) He spoke impeccable English when he greeted me.

"Did you have a good day today, Pana Lady Teacher?"

"I got lost many times but found a Piekania in Rynek and had a hot chocolate."

"Aha! No, no, no, don't go there, it's only for tourists, too expensive." He then whipped out a stack of business cards from his pocket and pushed one over the counter to me.

"Here! This authentic Warsaw cake and hot chocolate, much cheaper, better, say Piotor recommended it to you, Okay?"

With that, he smiled, bowed his head and turned his attention to the next guest. I giggled at my new status of 'Lady Teacher' and took the card gratefully. I'm sure he was paid a commission for introducing trade to local business, or it was a relative's place. Whichever it was. It turned out in the future to be a go-to place for a comforting treat!

Following a relaxing bath and freshen up, I felt fatigued, and so I decided to pass on a carbohydrate-laden dinner. After watching a confusing five minutes of incomprehensible Polish TV, I pulled up the duvet and set my alarm as I remembered my teaching mentor was calling to escort me to the language school. I also quickly wrote a little note to my daughter and drew her a picture of my new fur hat, ready to slip into the school post.

An early night after so many new experiences.

I was nervously excited about making my introductions the next day and hoping I'd eventually make some new friends. I drifted off to sleep after one last glance at the Warsaw skyline, the bejewelled lights bouncing off the snow that had started to fall again.

CHAPTER 6

Introductions & Misunderstandings

Graham, my mentor, reminded me of a slightly faded hippie. He wore unfashionably floppy hair and had a straggly ginger beard. His clothes, although appropriate for the harsh winter, were all in earth tones giving him the appearance of a slightly muddy professor.

However, this was only a first impression. After a few minutes of ice-breaking chat, he proved to be a very erudite, clever, chap, and I relied on him as a source of information and a walking networker with all sorts of ex-pats across the city. He was simply a treasure trove of contacts.

As we travelled together on the new metro system out into the inner city and Old Town where the Language School was based, he gave me a further batch of tram tickets.

"Best buy two weeks' worth at a time; it works out more economical; there are loads of kiosks in the city to purchase them. I must stress, though, that the Police and Tram Inspectors are VERY strict. You'll easily spot them; they are about 7ft tall.

Massive, like rugby prop forwards but with an air of thuggery!" He pointed to one that hopped onto the tram we were riding. "Told you." He whispered.

"I've seen real physical arguments on trams where people try to ride for free. So, make sure you always get your tickets punched with the date/time stamp as soon as you step inside the tram." He paused, looking around to make sure the man-mountain of an Inspector was out of earshot.

"Also, we'll give you a booklet of receipt sheets for our contract taxi firm; these are for assignments outside of the city where you can't yet reach by Metro. Out into the suburbs at Ustanow, one or two of our top clients have their main HQs miles away!" He smiled.

"Such…Such a lot to take in." I stammered nervously.

My head was reeling - trams, tickets, thugs, hmmm, I mused, I really missed my car at that moment.

However, when I looked out of the tram window at the gridlock of polluting traffic along the main Warsaw highways, I realised I wouldn't have coped with driving in this city. The early morning smog of misty pollution was already irritating my chest. I had to watch catching colds at the best of times after suffering from pleurisy from living in damp student digs years ago.

Now, this was like a harsh-winter climate with a great dollop of traffic pollution whipped into the air. I made a mental note to boost my immune by eating healthier. Clearly, eating chocolate cake and Kiabasa sausage every day was not the way to go!

I learnt that the Polish diet at that time was still heavy with carbs but quite healthy with vegetables. Since the influence of Western consumerist society and the infection of take-away outlets, I'm not so sure, but in the late '90s, it was still healthy soups, pierogi and bigos, hunter-meat stews.

I actually remember the media frenzy when Warsaw had its first McDonald's restaurant. The queues were legendary. Everyone who had aspirations to become more 'Western' wanted a burger!

There were always beautiful seasonal fruit and vegetables available in the shops and supermarkets. In the summer months, farmers and their womenfolk would sit by little stools with big paniers of ripe fruit and vegetables by major tram stops. It was fresh and perfect to eat THAT day.

My favourites were the cherries, nuts, strawberries, and whole sunflower seed heads quartered up for sale. That was a sight, watching well-groomed Warsovians on their way to work, snacking on sunflower seeds as they travelled by tram. The floor of the trams looked like the bottom of bird cages!

The English are considered great tea drinkers, and I think the Poles are as well, all sorts and varieties of tea. Every combination of fresh fruit and vegetable juices too. When I thought about it, they didn't waste their money on expensive, synthetic vitamins and mineral supplements. They consumed their fruit and vegetables in far greater quantities than the average Brit in their purest form to help their immune systems.

I ate far healthier once I'd settled down to my Warsovian lifestyle, the fruit and vegetables fresh and perfect to eat without storing for days on end in a fridge.

As we arrived at the International Language School where I'd be contracted to teach Business English, my stomach started to churn with nerves. This was going to be a formal introduction to the school Owners, Secretarial staff, and my colleagues in the TEFL department.

I frantically reached into my bag for my trusty Polish phrasebook. I wanted to make a good impression, and manners dictated I at least greeted with, 'Hello, pleased to meet you' in Polish.

I remember I felt a bit tatty and grimy as I was introduced to the glamorously groomed school secretaries. Not a cardigan in sight here. Elegant, reed-slim, young women in business power suits, heels, and full make-up. I felt a bit dumpy and frizzy. I made another mental note to smarten up my game with the business attire in future!

I was ushered into the owner's very plush, contemporary office. It had two huge mahogany desks, back to back, positioned in a light-filled, airy, high-ceilinged room.

The owners were a husband and wife team. Marcin, a strikingly tall, attractive man with salt and pepper hair, very dark eyes like coals, and an expensive grey silk suit. Agnieska, a diminutive painted doll. Everything about her was dark. Shiny bob haircut, dark eyeshadow, dark painted lips, dark power suit. Frankly, she looked like a well-polished Goth.

"Bardzo mi Milo." I announced boldly, shooting out my hand to shake each of them in turn.

"Oh! Well done, a perfect accent Ellie!" Marcin exclaimed as he pumped my hand, then grabbed and kissed the back of it! It was a very quaint Polish custom that men still used in formal introductions.

"That's a good start, Pana Ella." Agnieska purred as she gripped my hand and shook it very strongly. She was an Alpha female, and she was making sure I knew it immediately. It was a handshake that said, I'm in charge here.

Marcin wheeled me around and escorted me down the corridor to the large staffroom to introduce me to the central nervous system of the school. It had a large reprographics department, and the whirring and churning of the photocopies created a background hum to the following introductions. In all my time at the school, I hardly ever heard that machine silent, and it gave off plenty of heat in the process. I found it to be the place we all loved to congregate and gossip about Agnieska.

The warm, spacious staff room resembled a cross between a library and a Starbucks coffee shop. Professional coffee machines, textbooks and coloured papers were scattered around on desks. Large squishy leather sofas angled in cabal corners made it perfect for plotting and bitching about the Management.

It soon became apparent that Agnieska was a darkly scary powerhouse of a woman who used the words 'pedagogical processes' a lot in her meetings. Other teachers would do air quotes after she'd given another one of her pedagogical speeches to the staff.

A couple of teachers were heads down at a huge desk trying to lesson-plan; they looked up briefly. The next couple of hours were a blur of signing the paperwork for insurance, collecting locker-keys, entry passes, tram carnets, taxi receipt books and a lanyard with my photo ID.

I was shown the school canteen where they were preparing a hot lunch. It was cheap, nutritious, and hand-prepared fresh in the kitchen daily. Nothing was shop-bought. I particularly liked the soups and stews when I was on-site lesson planning in the winter months. The food was tasty and filling.

The two secretaries on reception spoke impeccable English with only a slight accent. I later found out that both had lived in the UK after going to university in London. One of them handed me a sheet of A4 with a list of school contacts and telephone numbers. Then another list with contacts for rental properties in the city.

They said they would dedicate some time every week to help me find an apartment as it would get expensive staying in the hotel for more than a month. Within the first two weeks, I had exhausted their list of contacts. My every spare moment was spent traipsing around the city on trams trying to find and view places. To be fair, it wasn't the Language School at fault; I was just very picky about my space.

The school had given me a very light teaching schedule for the first week or two. Just a few well established classes at the Language School to ease me into the system.

After a couple of weeks, I quickly settled into my new routine at the Hotel Polonia. I would breakfast early in the theatre-dining room, chatting very briefly with Piotor, the Concierge; he would usually give me a catalogue of business cards daily for this cafe or that cake shop. I got the feeling his extended family must have owned every eatery in the city. No doubt he got a commission for his soft lead generation.

There were a couple of funny situations that happened to me whilst I was staying at the Polonia in the early days.

The first was a laundry incident.

I'd bought enough clothes for a couple of weeks to get me started. I'd been so occupied and busy each day that the laundry pile built up, and I had no clean underwear, so I hand-washed an emergency supply to fill the top of the large radiator in my room, but I also needed a service wash.

The trusty phrasebook was whipped out when I had the first opportunity to chat to a Housekeeper as she knocked to clean my room.

I ran my finger down the phrasebook to a word I had assumed meant 'laundry' and held up a pair of knickers. The poor woman shook her hand and looked quizzical.

'No Laundry Service?' I wailed, flapping my big pants in surrender. Heck, I'd have to venture out and BUY some new underwear; that was going to tax my very basic language skills to the max; I really didn't want to spend hours hunting down new knickers!

'Surely, the hotel did laundry?' Blank stares I then tried phonetically spelling out the word I thought was laundry in Polish…"C-zy-sz-cz-z-en-ie na sucho?" I spoke slowly like to a child.

Suddenly there was a flash of recognition! She nodded enthusiastically, smiled and gave a thumbs-up. Grabbed my bag of unmentionables and scuttled off to clean the bathroom.

I positively looked forward to returning back to the freshly swept room and delicious smelling underwear. I need good hygiene practices in my life. Clean pants by lunchtime! I was Mistress of the Phrasebook!

Imagine my surprise, when I returned later in the day and heard a knock at my hotel door. I opened expectantly to find the Housekeeper holding a group of little hangers with each of my pants held in place, with tiny little pegs all covered in plastic sheathing. Fifteen pants starched flat and pegged out!

"What the…?" I groaned, then broke out into fits of giggles!

The Housekeeper had a massive belly laugh too, and pushed past me to the phrasebook on the bed. Running her finger down the lists, she pointed to the English translation, 'Dry Cleaning'.

Dry Cleaned Pants!

We both carried on crying with laughter. She shook her head and put her hand on my shoulder in sympathy, and continued down the list to 'laundry'. I at least had learnt a new word that would stick in my brain forever. My humiliation complete, I tipped her a few Zloty and carried on laughing out loud whilst I hung up my rolled, and stiff parachutes.

A couple of weeks later, just before I was about to move into my new apartment in the city, I had another embarrassing incident as I came home late from a lesson at the Language School.

It was particularly cold, and I'd swapped out my trusty all-weather jacket for my very long, sweeping, cashmere wool coat.

It was a very glamorous affair, stylish in a military embellishment way and grazed the tops of my thick-soled black patent leather boots. Coupled with my 'looks-like-a-rabbit' grey fur hat, I could have been mistaken for any stylish Warsovian woman.

It would have looked ridiculous in London, but in Warsaw, I looked Eastern European.

This particular evening, I'd caught the tram from just outside the Language School towards the hotel. However, at the tram stop, I bumped into a new teaching friend, Marzena, who persuaded me to go with her, to a new cocktail bar in the Old Town.

I'd been living like a sober Judge and hadn't had the opportunity to check out any nightlife on my own. Firstly, I would have felt self-conscious walking into a bar on my own, and secondly, I'd not mastered enough Polish to order alcoholic drinks. I jumped at the chance to go with her.

We arrived at a small bar off a main thoroughfare. It was a noisy, warm, crowded, but beautifully decorated bar. It definitely had an air of Speakeasy decadence about it.

My colleague, Marzena, ordered an aperitif that was a Warsovian favourite. A jug of freshly squeezed apple juice, two small glasses, and WHOLE bottle of Zurbrovka Vodka!

The Warsovians could often be seen, sitting at bars with jugs of juice and bottles of vodka. The system was pretty efficient; you paid for each quarter amount of the whole bottle. It meant you could have as strong or as weak an aperitif as you chose.

Marzena sloshed a drop of apple juice into each glass and poured obscene amounts of vodka over it. She knocked it back like shots, time, after time after time. I really enjoyed the taste of the 'Bison Grass' Polish vodka. It had a definite fresh flavour compared to the rough Russian paint-stripper, you could buy in plastic bidons at most 'Sklepy'.

Two hours later, having eaten only a few table snacks to soak up some of the booze, and with only a dribble of vodka left in our bottle, it was time to retire to my hotel. Feeling very light-headed and completely impervious to the biting cold temperatures outside, Marzena and I waited for a tram. She shared part of the journey and reminded me what stop number I needed to make, to get to the hotel nearby.

I could barely focus, the fresh air made my head spin, but I managed to ding the bell for my stop. I gathered as much dignity as I could muster, to not trip off the tram, and headed for the steps of The Hotel Polonia.

I managed the first few steps up to the revolving door of the hotel, when suddenly, I was trapped between the angled panes of glass!

I started to bang on the glass, then shouted. I caught the eye of a tall, gangly youth, not Piotor, on Reception. He wore the same style of Concierge uniform and was obviously in charge of the night desk.

I waved my arms at him, and he waved back, but in a dismissive way and proceeded to look down at his desk. I waved and banged hard on the glass,

"Prosimy! Propoze PROSIMY!" I yelled. I was properly stuck fast and starting to panic. I couldn't understand why he wasn't rushing up to help me to sort the door out.

"PROSIMY!" I shouted one last time.

To my astonishment, this young dolt told me to go away!

"IDA STAD." He barked and waved me off!

"Oi!…You little FUCKER…Open this door, you TWAT!…HELP ME!" I shouted in as plain Anglo-Saxon as I could muster.

The look on that young man's face drained of colour, and lo and behold, the door became unstuck after he pressed a button behind his desk. He suddenly realised with horror, that I was a guest and English.

"WHAT THE ACTUAL FUCK?" I screamed at him.

All politeness had evaporated in my freezing glass tomb. Cue much head-bowing and "Apologies Madam", in stilted English from the gangly Concierge.

It transpired that he thought I was one of the glamorous, 'ladies-of-the-night' that would visit guests, in all the Warsaw tourist hotels to provide 'services' to a steady stream of international visitors. I knew it went on, because every few days, a bright, glossy business card would be shoved under my hotel door.

The young Concierge thought I was a Hooker!

I didn't know whether to be offended or to congratulate myself that I looked Polish and beautiful enough to be considered a high-class TART!

As soon as I finally fell into my hotel room, I giggled to myself and collapsed onto the bed, boots, coat and hat and all, only to wake up in the early hours with the 'rabbit hat' suffocating me!

By breakfast, a hand-written note (in English) had been shoved under my door, formally apologising about the incident and offering me a free dinner on the house. Of course, I accepted and for the next week, whilst the young Concierge was on shift, I stuck my nose in the air and swept past him imperiously, resolutely refusing to talk to him.

How dare he! I thought, but secretly, I felt it gave me an air of superiority which I milked for all it was worth!

CHAPTER 7

Flat Hunting

The day-to-day reality of living in a hotel room felt claustrophobic after a month.

I was settling down, gaining confidence travelling about the city using the Metro and trams and making new friends. I wanted to start to socialise and invite people back to my own place.

It felt like being confined to a smart but faded barracks. The ever-watchful Concierge catching my eye, father-like or upstart novice, depending on who was on shift at Reception. I was either embraced and wafted through like a long-lost friend or sneered at with contempt. I'd had enough of living in a goldfish bowl.

It was time to find an apartment. The Language School had assigned a Secretary to spend some time each week to help me research and make arrangements to visit several available rentals within my budget. I didn't want to be outside the city limits, stuck out in the ever-developing new towns of existing drab suburbs. I didn't want extra traipsing and travel costs. I also wanted some cultural experiences, nightlife, bars, restaurants and city buzz.

After three weeks, I could start to hear a little frustration creep into the Secretaries' tone of voice.

"Really? Pana Ella? Other teachers have used this address previously; they liked it. Near a tram stop and only 40 minutes from the City...the room m² are larger than in the city, you sure?"

The square meterage of the average Warsovian City apartment was relatively small, about 40m², and at the time, would have been around $350 per month. Utilities were about $50.

I was paid in dollars from the Language School, not the local Zloty currency of the late 1990s. Compared to British teaching salaries, it was lower, but the cost of living was significantly cheaper. Rent, utilities, transport, and food especially, so my $1500 monthly salary stretched a long way. Frankly, I had a lot of disposable income; I lived like a queen. I visited the Kino (Cinema) every week, restaurants/bistro's several times a week and could save up enough for my daughter to visit me in the school holidays.

Agnieska's reputation preceded her. A note had circulated around the staffroom the previous week about certain operational procedural changes at the school. One wag had crossed out and written over the heading.

'By Order Of ~~Management~~ (The Diminutive One)'

Graham had spotted it and had screwed it up and thrown it in the rubbish bin, muttering something like, 'good job she didn't see this'.

My heart was pounding a little harder when I arrived at the school offices and was ushered into Agnieska's office by one of the secretaries, who put her hand on my shoulder and said, "Good luck Pana Ella." I felt sick, like a naughty schoolgirl awaiting punishment.

I mean, what had I done exactly? I thought. Okay, I'd been a bit choosy about where I wanted to settle with my accommodation. But hardly a telling-off offence, surely?

I decided to be all breezy and upbeat as I walked into the room confidently across her highly polished parquet flooring.

Agnieska came up to 4'9" in her ankle-breaking heels. Her polished raven black bob was perfectly coiffed. So perfect, I was starting to suspect it was a wig. She was immaculate, with not a crease, stain or speck about her person. By contrast, I schlepped in wearing jeans and trainers, a hand-knitted woollen tunic and the trusty Berghaus jacket.

"So, Pana Ella, we meet at last properly!" She purred and stretched out her doll-like hand with its blood-red talons towards an enormous leather chair in front of her tidy desk. The seat sagged as I plonked down. The effect was that I ended up peering up and over her desk. She however, perched, eyrie-like on her designer chair. A clever ploy to make darned sure you knew she was in charge.

"How are you settling down to life in Warsaw? Do you like it? I'm hearing good feedback from your students. You making friends yet?" She fired out rapid questions, hardly waiting for an answer.

"Yes, yes….er…all good, thanks! Working out better than I was expecting."

"Really? What were you expecting Pana Ella?" She pounced, her beady black eyes swivelled, boring into mine in a slightly interrogative stare.

"Well…er…I mean…um…I'm not too sure really (gulp) Er…perhaps I was expecting the city to be, I dunno, a bit drab….um…not like London anyway (nervous giggle)." I stammered; this woman made me nervous.

"Quite! Well you do know we are a free, progressive nation now, looking forward to the West, you understand? So let's get down to why I wanted to see you today. An opportunity has arisen within the team to work alongside a couple of our top clients. The executives want a more naturalistic language experience from a native English speaker." She droned on. "Tell me, Pana Ella, you have general business, working experience, do you not?"

"Oh yes, I've worked in general business management roles for a while now."

"Ah, good, so something like negotiating strategies, how to present proposals to senior board members, language connected with marketing terms, etcetera, etcetera."

"Oh!" I said in a surprised tone. "I thought you were going to mention that I haven't found an apartment yet!" I joked, and immediately regretted saying it.

She drew herself to my shoulder height and rubbed her head.

"Pana Ella, you really need to set up getting enrolled on our Polish language courses and finding an apartment. You're costing us a fortune in hotel bills!"

"Oh no, no…I'm paying my own hotel bill."

"Well, even more important you don't burn through your resources then." She said sharply.

"Sorry Agnieska, I'll be more focused this week then." I sounded like the naughty schoolgirl after all.

"So, getting back to my earlier suggestion, we'd like to offer you the newly created position of Business Course Development Manager; your business skills will be an asset to the School. Think about it; obviously, there will be a full package, and we can negotiate something with the Anglo-American School for your daughter if and when you bring her over. Okay? Let me know your decision next week!"

My head was reeling. Reprimanded and promoted within minutes of my meeting with Agnieska.

I felt a little dazed and went out for a drink after work with Marzena, to celebrate my good fortune. I had a new job title, a new role, and would soon have a little apartment, a base. Time to make some plans to sort out things for my daughter to come and visit me. I was starting to really miss her company, so when I returned home, I wrote her a little 'Bluey' sharing my news. I drew some silly sketches on the letter to entertain her.

Over the next couple of weeks, I made a concerted effort to really scour the details given to me by the secretaries, and I had a lucky break. A colleague working full-time at the Language School, teaching younger people, came up to me one lunchtime in the school canteen.

"Pana Ella, Marzena told me you're looking for an apartment in the city, is that right?"

"Yeah, I don't want anywhere stuck out miles away. Is it close to the School?" I asked hopefully.

"Oh yes. My girlfriend's just moved out, as she's working out near Imielin and wants to be closer to her new job. It's very central; it's opposite Saski Park, a bit small but nicely decorated; you want the Landlord's details?"

"Oh yes, that's fab; Thank you Pawel; I'm sure the secretaries will set a meeting up for me; cheers!" I beamed.

Thanks to the ever-efficient school secretaries, I visited the beautiful little apartment in the heart of the city. There was a tram stop literally opposite the beautiful Saski Park, where the Tomb of The Unknown Warrior was based. It had a parade of shops and a cafe at the base of a tall apartment block.

The apartment was twenty floors up, and I gasped with joy when I was led into the living room; it had a huge plate glass window with sheer floor-to-ceiling nets which revealed a stunning skyline. I looked out onto the district by the Place Bankowy. The former Bank of Poland. I could just see The Palace of Culture & Science to the left of the view.

The Landlord's son was apparently an artist. Every wall had original oil abstract art on it. Great reliefs of dried swirling oils. I had my own mini art gallery; they would definitely be a talking point if I ever had guests to visit.

It was small, even by Warsaw standards. However, the decor was lovely and airy, a perfect foil for the colourful art. The furniture was quality, with built-in cupboards in every room plus an ingenious sofa bed that I had to make every evening, but it only took seconds and packed away, bedding and all very neatly. The apartment came fully furnished, with all linens beautifully ironed and pressed in a cupboard in the dining room.

I was expecting to have to shop for those things, so it was a delightful bonus!

It had a compact shower over a sizeable bath and the space doubled as a utility wash room with a washing machine and drier, a definite plus. However, there was a laundry for the block on the ground floor.

The galley kitchen was tiny, but again, had clever space-saving touches and good equipment. It felt homely and stylish and was bang in the centre of the city. Just what I'd held out for!

I agreed the rent and paid the first month in cash there and then. Then spent the weekend moving my belongings over and exploring the district.

The first night sleeping on my comfy sofa bed, I drew the curtains back and stared at the lovely twinkling skyline of Warsaw. I was feeling excited that, at last, I had my own space. I no longer felt like a 'tourist'. It was time to breathe and start living again.

Spring was coming; green shoots were emerging on every street corner, maybe just maybe, this big gamble would work out for me!

CHAPTER 8

Vodka & Y2K Malarky

The leading brand of Polish Vodka at the time was 'Zurbrovka'- Bison-Grass vodka. Inside each bottle is a long blade of grass which imparts the vodka with a uniquely fresh 'green' taste. In my opinion, it's a delicious addition. It's often used as an aperitif with fresh apple juice.

In most bars, you'd get waiter service, and it would be brought to your table with the bottle plonked down, plus glasses and a jug of apple juice. The bottle may have been opened previously; you just served yourself! In the early days, I was far too generous in what I thought a measure of vodka was.

One humiliating incident I recall was after a 'sesh' with colleagues at the Language School. I'd had far too much to drink and needed 'escorting' by a work colleague who gallantly offered to get me home. I didn't make it easy for my poor friend in fact, I was quite belligerent, insisting that I'd be perfectly fine just to be shoved onto the next available tram!

"God! You're not my dad, y'know!" I snorted when he had the temerity to tell me to straighten up.

"Christ-sakes, you look a proper lush." He snapped as we started walking out, propped up together like a weird sack-race couple.

He escorted me to my new apartment, thankfully close to the tram stop at Plac Bankowy. As soon as he opened the door, I stumbled in, and all I remember, before I slumped over my bed was, he shouted.

"Drink some water!"

Hours later, I woke up in the dark room, freezing cold. I went to move off the bed and realised, too late, that my foot was wrapped around the strap of my handbag; I tripped and spreadeagled across the living room floor. There and then, I made a vow not to get myself into such a state again.

I'd made myself vulnerable, and I was a mum, for heaven's sake, not a teenager!

It didn't stop me from drinking Zurbrovka again; I loved starting to socialise and meeting my young colleagues from work at various fashionable city bars, the buzz and the nightlife atmosphere around the Old Town Starego Miasta. It had an alluring atmosphere, and old-world charm re-created strolling along its historic streets.

Drinking vodka was a very sociable activity in a very sociable city. It oiled the wheels of life, and I'll admit it, assuaged the gnawing loneliness I'd sometimes feel in my new apartment after working hours.

I was a little older than most of my younger colleagues, and I had parental responsibilities. Marzena and I were the only single mums on staff.

I wasn't the bright young thing I used to be before I had my daughter. Sometimes I'd sit after work in my apartment, and after I'd done some lesson prep, watched some unfathomable TV, done a quick tidy or laundry, it could be very quiet and lonely.

I'd write a little letter or try and call home on my new mobile phone to ease the growing homesickness; often, I'd just start to cry when I glanced at my daughter's perfect little face framed next to my bedside.

Years later, during a conversation a cousin had with my dad, she revealed what he'd said about my stint abroad.

"I just don't understand how she could have left Rebecca and gone galivanting over to Poland!"

When I learned this, it made me sad, that no one had really understood how I'd had to escape, get away, change tack in my life. I was grieving for the first marriage; even though it had broken down, it had been happy in the early years.

I felt brave and courageous for the first time in years; travelling alone and getting a job overseas was no mean feat. It had been a competitive task. Rebecca was too young to understand my reasoning, and was heavily influenced by what my parents and her father said about my time overseas.

Although I've constantly said I'll be forever grateful to my Mum and Dad at the time, for offering a home to us and allowing me a few months of freedom, the process did undermine my own parenting skills with Rebecca in subtle ways.

So, if I had too many Zurbrovkas in the early days, it was to blot out some of those deeply hidden emotions that would surface from time to time.

Once opportunities in life started to present themselves, I got used to manoeuvring around the city more expertly. I didn't feel the need to use Zurbrovka as a crutch and made far healthier choices, even when there was an air of apocalypse and excitement in equal measure as 1999 wore on.

The excitement of experiencing a new Millennium gripped the nation, in fact, the world in 1999.

Doom-mongers in the media had predicted that computers wouldn't cope with the new digits, from two to four. It's hilarious in hindsight, but reams and reams of column inches were written about how aeroplanes could drop out of the sky, ships go off course, and there was a complete neurosis, that people wouldn't be able to switch on their computers, or the screens would be blank!

'Y2K Is Coming!' was a familiar headline. 'Y2K', meaning the Year 2000.

Banks, companies, retailers, transport, the entire interconnected nature of the global economy, would end up in an apocalyptical nightmare.

I remember vividly, my daughter being so excited about finding out she was a 'Millennial' as she was born in '92. She told me in a very authoritative voice, that this was 'her' century and was very enthusiastic about her future life as a grown-up living on a Moon colony.

It was like some people had a wildly utopian sense of a bright shiny new century, whilst others had dystopian views about everything in society breaking down.

Every language course incorporated lessons to do with these issues, and the conversational language associated with new industries, space travel, and computers. I even remember reading a very fanciful account in a newspaper, which predicted the use of electric cars within a couple of years of the new century.

There was no end of fruit-cake predictions espoused by the chattering classes and neo-technocrats. One of my classes, filled with highly trained mechanical engineers and serious technical managers, would often chatter about it.

One day, I set a conversational task to the group to discuss what they would predict might happen after midnight on December 31st, 1999.

I also asked them to seriously consider what would happen, if it all turned out to be a damp squib. I was met with blank stares.

"What is this damp squib, Pana Ella?"

Oh no! An off-the-cuff colloquialism made me flounder for the right sort of language a non-native English speaker would understand.

A squib, is an old Navy term for an explosive. The squib needed to be protected from moisture. Thus a 'damp squib' would have failed to ignite. It later came to mean a disappointment or anti-climax. It is a particularly British slang word.

The same wag that had commented about food idioms was in the class and saw his opportunity to create more mayhem, in this classroom now.

"Pana Ella, you mentioned damp squibbles?"

"No, Marcin, a d-a-m-p s-q-u-i-b." I clearly enunciated.

"Oh yes, yes! Could I say, if my girlfriend didn't have orgasm after lovemaking, you have damp squib, Marcin?"

I was speechless! He had a twinkle in his eye and exchanged a glance with a colleague sitting next to him. He understood the context full well. The whole class erupted with laughter, and when his friend very dryly said, "My wife would never say I was damp squib in bed, huh!"

I just corpsed, and lost my composure; tears of laughter rolled down my cheeks. I gripped the desk gasping for air and let out a huge cackle which ignited even more racket from these very childish engineers.

However, I had the secret satisfaction of knowing that when these highly paid professionals were in business meetings at executive level, they could confidently use the phrase, "The Y2K hype is a complete damp squib", knowing their American counterparts, wouldn't have understood a word.

CHAPTER 9

Cowboys

One of the most left-field experiences, I had during my time in Warsaw happened on a beautiful spring Saturday morning.

I'd popped into the Rynek Starego Miasta (Old Town Square) for a touch of sightseeing, possibly a cake and coffee, at my favourite Cafe Blikle. Just to absorb the sights and smells of Warsaw blossoming and accepting tourists, after the brutal snowy hibernation.

There were many jewellery shops in the Old Town selling amber jewellery. Much of it was too expensive to buy casually, although I did eventually purchase a beautifully delicate, bracelet for my daughter. On this Saturday, I was content to just browse and press my nose to the window pane, admiring the exquisitely crafted and avant-guard patterns and shapes.

I sat in the Square at one point, listening to bells from a parish church somewhere peeling for a wedding procession. It was cheery, hopeful, and sitting there with the sun on my face, so was I.

This made me feel much less homesick. I'd really experienced the full force of searing homesickness, a couple of months after arriving in Warsaw. I was told by Graham, my mentor, to expect it.

"Usually kicks in a few weeks after the excitement and newness of the situation wears off; winter grinds on in its depressingly dreary way, just letting you know, its…er…common. We're all here to help you get through it; we'll take you out and about or call around for a chat. Just let us know, okay? Don't suffer in silence, or you'll be on a plane going back home too easily."

The week previously, my daughter had started to cry when I spoke to her on the mobile phone; she was starting to feel the separation more keenly too.

"But why can't you just come home now Mummy?" She sniffed.

It made my heart bleed, and I felt like a completely shitty mother. However, my Mum assured me that five minutes after getting off the phone to me, she'd perk up, especially if Mum distracted her with her favourite foods, reading stories or persuading her Grandad to take her to the toy shop down the road.

Separation was hard sometimes, but both of us could be distracted easily out of the fug.

I was reminiscing about all of this while waiting at my tram stop to go home. Trams were the fasted form of public transport crisscrossing the city, east-west, north-south. My tram would wind around the Old Town and, within ten minutes, would deposit me a hundred yards away opposite my apartment block in Plac Bankowy.

The tram approached, rumbling to a shuddering stop; the doors swooshed open, and an enormously tall, young chap jumped out of the middle doors; I glanced at him as I queued to enter at the front. He was dressed in a denim jacket with a fur collar, a Stetson hat and had a canvas rucksack slung across his shoulders.

He caught my eye, smiled, and immediately came up to me without any preamble or asking if I could speak English! He just launched,

"Hello Ma'am. Could you tell me if I'm anywhere near Aleja Zerolimskie?" He pronounced every letter, so it sounded like A-l-e-j-a Z-e-r-o-l-i-m-s-k-i-e

"Er. Hello. Well, I'm about to go past there on this tram home; you need to pop back on; you're going in the wrong direction if you get off; quick, get back on; I'll give you a nudge where to hop off!" I giggled.

The relief flooded through him, and he flashed a dazzlingly wide grin with perfectly white teeth back at me.

"Wow! Ma'am, you speak English real good!" He bellowed.

I couldn't help myself; I replied, "I speak English really well!"

As he clambered on board again, he fumbled with his ticket carnet; and we found an empty 'end' that was for standing room only that had sturdy handrails running around at about waist height to hold on to.

He smiled shyly as I asked, "Tell me, what is a big American chap like you doing in Warsaw? You look like a Cowboy!"

" Ma'am, I'm from Texas; my name's Jim, by the way." He shot out a hand the size of a large rump steak, all calloused, but with beautifully manicured nails.

"Hello Jim, I'm Ellie," I responded, sounding very prim. "So Jim, again, why are you here? You seem like a fish out of water!"

He grinned, flashed his kilowatt smile, lowered his head and half-whispered, "I'm here to take part in an International Bartenders Convention."

My disbelief must have registered because he quickly explained,

"I work on a small family farm ranch back home; it's self-sufficient, but to help pay the bills, I do shifts in the local bar in town for extra income, and cuz, I like it.

"Got into the cocktail-making side of things for the ladies. Have you ever watched the film 'Cocktail' with Tom Cruise in it? Well, my boss said we could do with some of that showing-off to bring in more customers. Without braggin', I had the best flair, so we gave it a go; pretty damned successful with those gals! He guffawed

"Saw this thing as a bit of an adventure, had to have a competition Stateside to get in, and here I am!"

He was obviously so excited I had to ask, "How big is this event then?"

"Oh, should attract several hundred people tonight!"

"How many? I've not heard anything about it; I'm missing a trick here obviously!" I laughed.

"Hey! Did you wanna see me perform tonight? Got some extra tickets, my Uncle came out with me. Err…you could bring a friend? We need more support!"

"Oh Jim, really? That's kind of you; hmmm, why not?" I said enthusiastically.

He rummaged through his rucksack and produced a couple of brightly printed tickets to the event. I'd just thanked him when I looked out and noticed his stop was rapidly approaching.

"Oh right, err, your stop is coming up Jim; I'll ding the bell. When you get off, it's about 100yards on the right-hand side. The hotel is on the corner; you can't miss it!' I'll drag a pal of mine out with me; we'll give you a cheer!"

"Aww Thank you Ellie; see you around 7pmish? There's a bar before the main entrance; we'll be milling around before they call us in. Thanks again." He tipped his hat, gave a flash of the killer smile, and hopped off the tram, striding down Aleja Zerolimskie.

Blimey! What a weird and unexpected encounter, I thought as I studied the tickets he'd handed to me; it did indeed say 'International Bartenders Convention, 1999.'

I resolved to phone up Marzena. Neither of us went out much in the evenings, but I had an intuitive feeling, that she'd be persuaded to ask her Mum to baby-sit for a girlie night out. Watching a Cowboy from Texas, with the added bonus of drinking cocktails!

CHAPTER 10

Cocktails

By the time I'd reached my stop at Plac Bankowy, the beautiful old Bank of Poland building, and the all-glass Blue Tower (site of the old Jewish Synagogue) were bathed in the dimming golden light of this perfect spring day.

I admit I was feeling a little smug with myself as I'd met a real Cowboy, and in Warsaw of all places!

However, by the time I'd reached my apartment in Prezechodnia, clambered into the rickety old lift and walked down the hallway to my place, I'd pretty much resolved NOT to attend.

What was I thinking? A Bartenders Convention?

It was all too weird, and I was tired from all the window shopping and walking around the Old Town.

Nope, a good shower, PJs, a good book, bed. Then I caught sight of myself in my full-length hall mirror. I'd realised I'd dropped a couple of stones in weight, I was trim, my hair was looking glossy and wavy, and my skin glowed.

I thought, 'You know what, I'm single, and I can do anything I want to; I'm not a ruddy Nun; I'm going out, out, out!'

Before I could talk myself out of it, I grabbed my mobile and called Marzena. I had to explain to her three times that it was a Bartenders' Convention; like me, she'd never heard of anything like it. She jumped at the chance but said she'd have to clear it with her mum, and she'd call me as quickly as possible.

Five minutes later, she said, "I'm on my way; I've brought a dress for you Pana Ella."

"Pardon? A dress? I've got a dress!" I said indignantly.

"Pah! That's okay for work. No, you need a better dress. I have loads; we're about the same size, anyway, you try it on? No? Do widzenia!"

She breezed by twenty minutes later, looking chic in a green tartan, white collared dress, and high black boots that showed off her elegant legs. She was classically beautiful, with high cheekbones, jet-black hair and striking, light blue eyes. She was also a flirt, and would likely cop off with someone she'd meet tonight, so mentally, I made a note and stuffed extra taxi fare into my purse.

"Oh my god! You're so English, you and your bloody jumpers! I'm not going out with you looking like that!" She laughed as she pointed to my sensible attire.

"All right, bossy-boots, give it here, and I'll attempt to squeeze into it." I huffed as I reached out for the dress.

I must admit the simple, cherry red shift dress was sexy and classy. A scarf worn at the neck and a pair of black courts looked better than my uniform sensible knits and jeans!

"C'mon Pana Ella, hurry up, we can get some Zurbrovka before we go to the hotel, rozumiem?"

"Yeah, yeah, I understand! Let me put some lippy on." I laughed as I quickly smoothed down the dress, popped the tickets in my handbag and linked arms with my new friend Marzena.

We were going out, out, out!

Fifteen minutes later, we emerged from the tram stop at Centrum and walked a hundred yards or so across the highway, the great Al. Jerozolimskie, one of the main arteries that cross the city east to west.

Dead ahead was the hotel. It was fairly new (mid-1990's and unapologetically deluxe, glossy and tall. As we walked through the impressive Grand Lobby, we could see many people carrying the flags of Poland, France, Germany, Netherlands, South Africa, Brazil, Japan, USA.

There was an enormous board edged in gold stating 'International Bartenders Convention 1999, 30th floor. Panorama Bar'.

Marzena grabbed my arm and guided me through to the sleek lifts, surrounded by marble and chrome. This hotel reeked with new wealth.

This was NOT one of the many tourist class hotels that had been converted from the days of the Polish People's Republic (basically for peasants and soldiers) or the many renovated garrison hotels occupied by officers of the former Warsaw pact countries.

No, this was post-modern, architecturally interesting and for the nouveau riche. Quite brash in fact.

"I've heard there are great views from the 'Panorama Bar'!" Marzena squealed excitedly as we huddled inside the lift. We swooshed up so quickly that my stomach lurched a little. The doors silently opened, and our senses were immediately assaulted.

As soon as we stepped into the small lobby of the 'Panorama Bar', we faced an enormous wooden-edged door with clear glass panels and brass handles. Muffled pulsating sounds could be heard from behind the door, and strobe lighting shone through. We looked at each other with wide-eyed amazement.

When we opened the doors, the noise was deafening! Throbbing lights with the thumping music meant we could hardly hear what the security guard standing just inside the entrance was saying.

He tapped Marzena's shoulder to attract her attention and said something unintelligible. She poked at my handbag to indicate, show the tickets. They were gathered in, and we had the backs of our hands stamped in dark blue ink. A very skinny, made-up doll of a woman smiled sweetly and guided us to the bar area.

Marzena partly screamed into my ear, "WE CAN GET A FREE DRINK BEFORE THEY LET US UP TO THE PANORAMA!"

"GOT TO BE A COCKTAIL," I shouted back.

We arrived just in time to get to the bar. Suddenly there was a scrum of people venturing up from the lobby and heading for the bar. Marina quickly shouted something in Polish to the woman behind the bar, and seconds later she produced two 'Margaritas'.

"Ella, take the drinks, take the drinks, quickly; WE NEED GOOD SEATS!" She shouted.

She wheeled me around and through the door leading to the Panorama. I drew a huge gasp, "Oh my god! Oh Wow, would you look at that!"

It was a beautiful cavernous space, surrounded by what seemed like a 360-degree Panoramic view of the twinkling Warsaw skyline. We were ushered to seats overlooking a huge glass bar with various cubicles along it. Rows and rows of glass shelves were groaning with brightly coloured bottles of booze.

Underneath the bar area were wooden crates with numbers on them. It had an arena feel about it all. Marzena was determined to get a good view of the proceedings. We were seated pretty much in the centre rows and were giddy with excitement. Then

I stopped and remembered I was supposed to meet Jim at the Lobby Bar!

Marzena wouldn't let me wander about trying to look out for him, and time was ticking. "No! Sit down Ella, we don't want to lose these seats, look it's filling up fast, think it's going to start soon! You can see him afterwards!"

It started to get noisy with lots of chatter, mostly Polish. However, I did hear snippets of other languages.

The view out of the panoramic windows was spectacular. Twilight sky of maroon streaks and twinkling lights shining brightly from monuments, tower blocks, hotels, and highways. Warsaw had never looked so amazing as far as I was concerned. From this viewpoint, it looked a little like Downtown Manhattan or parts of Canary Wharf in London. A glamorous view, for sure!

Another ten minutes and the place was heaving; an air of anticipation was felt, and then suddenly, music struck up. 'The Beat Goes On', an eighties dance floor filler, followed by a very tall Polish MC clutching a mic. The MC started off in Polish and then repeated in English. He introduced the event, something about it being the first of its kind being held in Poland, and a huge cheer and whistling went up.

He then started to introduce the contestants individually. In our haste to grab good seats, we'd forgotten to pick up a programme explaining more about the event and the Bartenders' biographical details.

I was craning my neck to look over to the two giant screens on either side of the bar area, where I was guessing the contestants were nervously waiting to be lined up. From what we could make out, there were twenty contestants, and Jim would be fourteenth in the line-up.

There was more up-tempo music as the MC came off the stage.

Soberly dressed contestants started to file across the stage area behind the long glass bar, standing in front of their little cubicles. They were all smartly dressed in dark trousers, white shirts and black waistcoats. I counted four female Bartenders. I clearly saw Jim as he was the tallest contestant and nudged Marzena to point him out.

"Oh, the tall one? Oh yes, I can see him; he's definitely my type!"

I rolled my eyes; that poor young man didn't stand a chance once Marzena had set her sights on him. Marzena had a few boyfriends in tow. She was technically still married. She had a very strict Catholic mother, so Marzena rarely had opportunities to bring her men-friends back home.

I've never forgotten the smell, excitement and imagery of this evening; I suppose it's why I still enjoy drinking cocktails today. The emotion and memory wrapped up in the drinks themselves.

The competition was divided up into several heats. The first two had all to do with the skills of Bartending. Heat One was 'Working Flair', and Heat Two was 'Craft Flair'.

To understand 'flair' in Bartending, we have to go back in time to before the advent of the 'Mixologist'.

Bartending had been made fashionable as a highly-paid working-class job back in the 1980s. Made glamorous even by the film 'Cocktail' starring a very young Tom Cruise.

The characters who tended bars, initially in the US, became famous for their flashy moves and skilled pouring artisan cocktails.

Skill and art form, combined with showmanship, gave the customer 'value added' entertainment at their fashionable bars and restaurants. The simple truth was it appealed to the growing trend for women to go out drinking away from the home.

We settled down to watch all the contestants deal with the craft of Bartending, laying out napkins, garnishing, and ice skills, all sexed up with sleight-of-hand moves to pulsating beating music.

All the contestants were lined up behind the bar, divided by a Perspex screen of about twelve inches high. Six International Judges were positioned around the front, all wearing headphones and furiously scribbling notes every few seconds.

The heat was pretty quick, but I did pick up a tip or two about chopping ice (for an 'Old Fashioned' drink, it has to be shaped from one lump) and how to set fire to orange peel to release the essential oils for an instant hit of citrus aroma.

Marzena was transfixed; she'd admitted she'd never visited this hotel before as it 'was International and too pricey for a working person'. She had a point; our two cocktails, if we had paid for them, would have cost an hour's wage.

We wouldn't be getting drunk or even tipsy at this hotel. Before the commencement of the second heat, we scampered off to the ladies and topped up our glasses with plain tap water to hydrate.

There was more pulsating music, and counters cleared for the next round - Exhibition Flair. It was a chance for Jim to show off his juggling skills. I hadn't realised that during a contest, Bartenders used special lightweight bottles, only one-third full of liquor. Trying to juggle a full bottle was tricky and would result in too much costly spillage.

We tried our best to make a noise and create some support for Jim.

He possibly had the least amount of support in the space. We did our best "whoop, whoop'" and shouted, "Go Jim!" We were enjoying ourselves more than we were expecting to.

Jim did look slick as he twirled, shimmied and poured his drinks behind the bar. He definitely had a bullish Texan confidence, plus that smile. He had a permanent grin on his face throughout his exhibition.

I remembered what he mentioned on the tram earlier about showing off to impress the 'ladies'. He got a gasp from the crowd when he made a 'tin-on-tin' move with the shakers. I don't know how he did it, but they were sort of stacked in an arc, all filled with liquor, a row of shot glasses were then all filled individually from each tin, all different colours.

It was a magical moment and a crowd-pleaser; we both shouted 'Yay!' self-consciously as he did a bow to finish his flair.

Cue more music, slick lighting and our host rattling on about the elimination rounds to produce the classic five cocktails.
Now, this was an education. From my direct experience of watching these fabulous Bartenders, I can make a good 'Old Fashioned' 'Martini', 'Daiquiri', 'Flip' and a 'Fizz'.

I can honestly say I fell in love with making cocktails and aperitifs for parties; I've always associated it with fun times, lady-like drinks and sophistication. No necking alcho-pops or craft beers for me, thank you!

We were surprised Jim got eliminated after this round; his dazzling smile hadn't been enough to help him through. He was a good sport and waved and blew kisses to the audience. He was still young compared to some of his fellow competitors, and I'd remembered he'd said he wanted to do it to gain more experience outside of the States.

I smirked to myself, thinking, imagine how impressed those American gals are going to be when you tell them you've been to Europe!

Marzena's' interest started to wane in the rest of the competition once Jim was eliminated, and she started fidgeting and looking around the 'Panorama Bar' to catch sight of him and his uncle. She obviously fancied him and insisted we snake our way down to where he was now seated to make our introductions before the final heats.

As we went down to floor level, we were handed a branded 'Kaluah' bag full of samples by a gorgeous young woman who was obviously employed to promote the brand. The haul included a bottle of coffee liquor, cocktail umbrellas, a cocktail jigger and recipe cards. I made a sign to have two bags so Marzena could have one as well.

We made our way to Jim's table; he recognised me; cue big hugs and back-slapping and introductions to Jim's uncle, who was probably in his late forties.

We all had a lovely evening, chatting, and laughing, and Marzena was flirting outrageously with Jim. I mean, she was a decade younger than me, so why not? I had zero interest in

Jim's uncle. Nice enough, but not my type, and he was a good decade older than me!

After another hour of watching the competition and chatting, overwhelming fatigued flooded over me. I made a sign to Marzena to say our goodbyes. She gestured over to the ladies' toilets. Once there, she said,

"Okay, you go home?"

"Yes, I'm getting really tired now."

"I'm staying! Jim is a sexy guy, don't you think Ella? Anyway, Jim wants to go onto a club, we get jiggy-jiggy maybe? You wanna go with his uncle?"

"Urgh, God, no! Nah, I'll grab a taxi, I brought extra fare with me. Are you going to be okay with these chaps?" I said with sudden concern.

"Ella! You're not my Mama! I'm okay. Okay?" She giggled.

Marzena, she came, she saw, she conquered poor Jim, I mused, Oh, to be twenty-something again!

"Lucky Jim!" I chuckled.

CHAPTER 11

Sexual Healing

The amazingly bonkers evening out, watching Bartenders make wonderful cocktails, with the lovely entertaining company, did change a few things about my social life after that.

I realised I didn't have a social life!

Marzena had spoken the truth, I wasn't her mum, and I was behaving like a nun.

I reminded myself that I was barely thirty-six years old. Compared to some of my fellow teaching colleagues, I was a little older, but I was newly single, attractive and without the daily care of my child.

I'd been in the city three months and hadn't so much as had a single date. A younger Australian teacher had tried to make some moves on me, but I didn't fancy him at all and was very 'cool' to all his approaches. I'd just concentrated on finding my bearings, coping with the language and making friends.

It was solidly into the spring season; the days were getting longer and warmer. The flowers were all blossoming in the parks, especially in Saski Park, opposite my apartment. As I stared at my bleak social calendar page, I resolved to get out and about more across the city and to make more connections.

Spring is a fairly short season in Poland, and it has Continental weather, unlike Britain. It means very defined seasons: a severe dry winter, short but bright damp spring, a very hot and humid summer, and a lovely mellow and warm autumn.

For a Celt like me, late summer and early autumn were the most pleasant of all, with no horrible biting mosquitos, but still able to wear light clothing in September.

However, I was grateful to see the leaden skies over Warsaw lighten up, and there had been a week leading up to Easter in early April when the weather suddenly warmed up. Slushy snow and biting cold arctic winds seemed to disappear to be replaced with benign warm breezes, weak sunshine and clear pale blue skies.

I enjoyed looking out from my large living room apartment window, watching the skyline change with the different light and shade, and the smells wafting from the flower market overlooking Solidarnosaci Square.

Solidarnosci was a political movement led by a Polish worker hero, Lec Walenska, in the late 1980s. He helped galvanise a people's revolution for freedom for the Polish people from the tired, controlling Soviet system imposed by the USSR.

The Square was enormous and dedicated to his memory. On public holidays or events, it could cram thousands into the space. Indeed, when Pope John Paul II visited in the summer of 1999, his last visit, a dais was erected in Solidarnosci Square for people to celebrate and congregate.

I was so lucky to be in Warsaw to experience his visit.

Whether you were a Catholic or not, he was a much-loved World figure and Polish by birth. He was treated like a rock star in the city. Young and old alike would wave the Polish and Papal flags and greet him with shouts of 'Witaj Tata' (Welcome Father), an informal address. I could actually see the Papal dais, all white and gold canopies, from my balcony; however, I watched the address on my little TV.

Just behind the square was one of my favourite haunts in the city, the flower market.

I'd gotten into a habit on late Saturday afternoons, of strolling from my apartment block over to the market, passing a little side street café for a delicious hot chocolate and then picking up armfuls of Freesias.

They were my favourite flowers, so cheap and plentiful; I bought a carrier bagful each week to put into a very modern round shallow vase in the apartment. Firstly, they looked stunning, and secondly, they emitted a lovely delicate fragrance throughout the whole space.

So, on a beautifully bright, spring, Saturday morning, I'd just had a catch-up phone call with my daughter; I was primed to be in a great mood for flower shopping. I set off and walked behind the Warsaw Town Hall onto the wide pavements of Aleja Solidarnosci leading towards Solidarnosci Square.

The sun was on my face, the blast of warm air made my spirit soar. I felt alive.

I was becoming happier inside myself; the homesickness was coming under control. I reminded myself I had an interesting and fulfilling job teaching; I had survived living and travelling about a new city and was creating some new routines. I'd learnt some survival Polish to travel and feed myself; however, my most used phrase was nie rozumien! (I don't understand).

Green shoots of life were beginning to form within me, life was feeling more vivid and exciting, and I knew I was on the cusp of new experiences. My instincts were fizzing with possibilities.

I've always believed that life is more interesting if you can share it with someone close, a lover or partner.

I was only just starting to put back the shattered pieces of my self-esteem and confidence. So not a full-on relationship as such, more a good time, a few laughs, dinner dates, and if it led to casual sex, so be it. I realised with a shock, that I hadn't actually had anything close to sex for about eighteen months!

I made up my mind; I wasn't going to appear to be the 'Ice Queen' at the Language School staff room anymore.

I really wasn't the type to hang out at bars by myself or to go clubbing. No, I'd just flirt a bit more. Unfortunately, my body completely betrays my feelings; I blush so easily. I'd perfected the art of fluttering my long lashes a bit, so with the limited tools at my disposal, I decided to get back out there!

One of the perks of my teaching role was that for several of my assignments outside the city centre, my travel was paid for.

The multinational client companies, had arrangements with various taxi firms. We were given a booklet of pre-printed receipts. The taxi drivers just had to date and sign the chits with the amount; each week, these were handed to the school secretaries who would deal with the invoicing. It meant I didn't have to fiddle around with currency when teaching.

I seemed to have the same taxi company for my trips, out to a large drinks company which was based outside the city on an industrial site.

If I'd had to visit there under my own steam, it would have taken forty-five minutes and two tram changes to get there. The taxi ride was usually about fifteen minutes. I could call up, and be picked up at the base of my apartment and dropped off directly outside the security gates.

The taxi drivers would hurtle at frightening speeds on the highways and then rat through housing complexes. I always wore a seatbelt! When I'd finished my assignment, I'd get one of the glamorous receptionists to phone the taxi company to pick me up.

Sometimes though, if I didn't have another teaching client to visit, I would make my own way home, taking the tram back through the winding routes of the Old Town (Starego Miasta) and wandering around the Royal Castle.

The Old Town was a beautifully reconstructed 'chessboard' of geometric medieval town planning. Completely razed to the ground in 1945 by the Nazis, It was rebuilt with pride and is now a UNESCO World Heritage site.

Rynek Stareo Miasta (Old Town Market Square) buzzes with restaurants, shops, and museums, leading to the old city walls and Barbican next to St. John's Cathedral, a tourist honeypot.

However, this story relates to a return, taxi journey from the drinks company.

I jumped into the back seat, and asked the driver to take me to my Language School in the city. He was someone who'd driven me before a few times, and we'd conversed on occasion. He was called Bogdan; I knew that, because it was on his ID in the taxi

.

His English was on the 'pidgin' side of proficiency, and he relayed that he loved "Manchester United Football Club, you like? I like - Beckham? He plays very good football, good, you know him? You know football?"

"Err, no Bogdan, I don't like football, actually I'm more of a Rugby fan!" I giggled.

A quizzical look appeared on Bogdan's face.

"What is this Rugaby?"

"R-U-G-B-Y" I spelt out.

He was none the wiser; he kept looking at me in the rear-view mirror, and I smiled back politely. I then noticed he smelt differently than when he'd transported me around on other occasions. He smelt rather delicious, like a mixture of spice and apples.

"Hmmm...you smell nice today Bogdan. Your scent? A-f-t-e-r-s-h-a-v-e?" I gestured to his face.

"You like? New!...For you!" He grinned.

"Me?" I immediately blushed.

Bogdan wasn't a young man; I was guessing he was in his mid-forties. He was tall, well over 6ft, well built, not fat exactly, but muscular and had a dark crew cut tinged with silver flecks at his temples. He had thick bushy eyebrows and dark brown eyes.

He always looked smart in his European uniform of freshly pressed light blue cotton shirt and navy slacks.

Then I noticed his tanned arms and large gold watch catching the spring sunshine. It looked like a Breitling watch. I have a thing about good watches. Whether it was real or a good imitation, it looked classy, and I liked that.

I had noticed these details in a split-second about him, and he had done likewise.

"You like this new scent, Pana?" He said, turning around to catch my eye.

"Oi, turn around Bogdan, eyes on the road!" I giggled. "Yes, I like it."

He nodded happily. Nothing else was said, and I thought nothing of the exchange until ten minutes later when he parked up outside the school. He swivelled around when I handed over my taxi chit to be signed.

"Give me your telephone number, please Pana?"

"Pardon?" I stalled

"You, pretty English lady, your number, eh? What is your name?"

"Oh, err, Ellie, Pana Ella." (It was easier to pronounce Ellie as Ella)

"So, your number Pana Ella?"

"Oh; really, umm, not sure about that Bogdan." I blushed.

"Why not? You want dinner, kino?" He pressed.

"Err - well - okay, dinner?" I said, my heart thumping.

I felt a bit weird. He clearly fancied me, and he wasn't unattractive.

I couldn't see him wearing a wedding band. That didn't mean he wasn't married though. I thought he'd mentioned going home to his mother in a conversation once, plus he never mentioned a wife or girlfriend in any chat. I had wanted to flirt more to test the water out, this was a result!

He was always friendly, and perhaps he wanted to practice his English speaking skills, I thought naively. Perhaps that was it; he wanted free language lessons!

"So, you want to practice your English speaking skills Bogdan?"

"No!" He snorted. "My English okay! No lessons. You want fuck?" He said matter-of-factly and shockingly direct.

I could feel the tsunami of red erupting from my neck up to my face.

He'd said the 'F' word. Actually, my body was screaming YES PLEASE! But as a nicely brought up gal, I stammered, "Oh B...Bogdan! So direct! Erm - well, let's start with dinner, shall we?" I giggled and fluttered my eyelashes.

"When you free Pana Ella?"

I wasn't going to say…TONIGHT!

I fumbled through my diary, couldn't say Friday in Polish, so I just shoved the diary in his face and pointed to the date.

"I take you to good restaurant in city; you'll like it. 8 pm. I smell good for you! Ha! Bogdan eats good!" He roared with laughter, showing good teeth.

This man had all his own teeth and hair and smelt good…it was promising!

Friday came, and I was taken to a restaurant that ironically sounded like 'Fuks' in the Old Town. It was beautifully rustic inside. There was soft lighting by candles, herbs and flowers all over the server, a traditional fireplace with cooking implements and traditional Polish folk music playing.

It was an assault on the senses and unashamedly Polish in its cuisine and style.

Bogdan was trying to impress me. I knew of this place from others at the Language School, so I also knew it was quite pricey. I said I didn't want a starter or dessert. He genuinely looked relieved but said we could share a cheesecake back at my place if we wanted an aperitif nightcap.

We all know what that implied and what 'nightcap' was code for.

That night, that man devoured me, just as we'd greedily eaten the cheesecake when we returned to my apartment. I didn't even make the sofa bed up. I'd broken my duck and didn't get a wink of sleep!

In the morning, he arose early because he had to work. He kissed me tenderly, "Dzien Dobry" (Good Morning), then coarsely said, "We do good fuck piatek (Friday) Pana Ella? We do fuck?"

I had been sensible and used protection.

I didn't know him very well. I still didn't know if he was married or had children; my Polish conversational skills hadn't allowed me to explore this.

If I'm honest, it was the perfect liaison; I had a regular shag on the next few Fridays. I wanted uncomplicated. Bogdan was an uncomplicated man; he just wanted lots of sex.

He offered me sweet and tender sexual healing, I felt feminine and wanted after my arid spell, but after a few weeks, although the sex was pleasurable, I started to miss conversation, to be able to go out on proper dates.

He never took me out to another restaurant or even to the cinema, kino. When I said it was time to stop seeing him, he shrugged and said, "Aw Pana Ella, you good for me, I good for you, we good in bed, no more talk of no going out!"

I stopped using that taxi company.

Many weeks later, he actually came out to the Language School to pick me up, but I refused to get in his taxi. He muttered something, thumped his steering wheel then drove off. He texted a couple of times, but I never saw him again.

Bogdan had, however, given me a healthy interest in the opposite sex again after my self-imposed period of celibacy. There must be a hidden radar or pheromone telegraph, around sexually active women. Suddenly, men were calling, attempting to chat with me and actually flirt.

I'd started to go out more with my teaching colleagues after work at weekends.

There were many popular pubs with the ex-pat community. Some Friday nights, there were wall-to-wall Aussies, Kiwis, and British chaps propping up the bars, eating polish sausages and downing copious amounts of Zywiec beer.

One night George, one of the TEFL teachers, joined our group without his girlfriend; she was always by his side like a limpet, pressed or draped over him in a possessive way. So when George sidled up to me with a beer in hand and offered it to me, he took me by surprise.

We started chatting, and we became flirtier and flirtier and merrier with each drink.

"So George, where's 'Paula' tonight?" I gestured in air quotes.

He bowed his dark blond head towards mine and whispered, "We're not an item anymore Ells!"

"Oh really? Awww, that's a shame; you looked good together." I lied.

He shrugged his shoulders, "It was getting too intense; she was giving heavy hints that we should make it more exclusive, settle down a bit. She even mentioned wanting a kid, not ready for all THAT!"

I felt booze-brave, fluttering my eyelashes. "What DO you want then, George?"

"Aha! Fuck knows Ells!" He said whilst turning his body away from the group and focusing his very dark brown eyes on me, pools deep enough for me to drown in.

"Ohh, steady-on George!" I giggled, a little off-guard with his directness.

I had noticed him immediately on the first day I was introduced to the staff; I'd guessed he was about my age; he was definitely more mature than the normal crowd.

He had been sitting by the large wooden desk in the staffroom doing his lesson planning. He'd looked up briefly and shook my hand, and I'd felt a fizz of energy immediately. He then smiled briefly and carried on with his task.

George was a career Teacher, not a gap-year TEFL. His father was Polish, and his mother Irish; he'd returned five years previously to care for his dad after his mother had passed away. He was quietly professional, suave and had Slavic bone structure and height mixed with Irish charm.

Although I'd felt some chemistry between us, I always thought he wasn't remotely interested in me because Paula had always been around.

She was Australian, late twenties, classically blonde and tanned, lithe, and loved the sound of her own voice too much. She had a really annoying tone to her voice that set my teeth on edge. I just didn't like the woman!

George whispered into my ear, "Do you want to go somewhere quieter?"

I quickly looked around me; no-one was paying us any attention. He left first, and I followed out onto the pavement glistening with fresh rain. He tapped me on the shoulder and said, "BOO!" which made me scream.

"Oooh! Ells, so jumpy! Did you want a proper drink at mine? Much cheaper, I'm not that far, five minutes, two if it rains again." He laughed.

I liked his affable, easy-going humour, so I trotted off with him. The minute we entered his apartment, I could smell something delicious.

"Oh what's that smell, an air freshener?"

"Air-freshener? I'm a bloke Ells! No potpourri here!" He snorted.

"What is it then, smells very fruity, floral?"

"Oh! It's the Rumptopt jar in the kitchen; I suppose I've got used to it. I topped it just before I went out; want a sample?"

"What is it?"

"Well, it's pretty common over here; it's a ceramic jar with a tap. You plonk in left-over fruits and bits of booze, I suppose it's a way of preserving fruit, but it gets mashed down into a sticky fruity firewater! A bit potent!" He laughed.

I gave it a good sniff; it nearly blew my head off and made my eyes water from the alcoholic fumes. I really should have known better.

About three drinks later, I was absolutely legless.

The room was swaying, and I ended up propped up on George's sofa. I awoke on the sofa at about 6 am with a thick blanket over me and in a blind panic. Where the hell was I? Oh, not again, Oh no, George! I was at George's. Oh, we didn't, did we?

Remorse flooded through me; please, please, dear God, don't let anything have happened that was inappropriate.

As I was coming around, George strode into the living room, all hale and hearty in a faded t-shirt and boxer shorts revealing tanned hairy legs.

"You okay there Ells? Still breathing? Bloody heck woman, you can drink and snore. Left you to it!" He roared with laughter.

At first, I was relieved, then mortified, then brassed off, and finally embarrassed.

"Oh gawd, sorry. It's all your fault and the Rumtotty-jar-thingy. Jeez, my head!"

"I'll get you some water and a paracetamol; you do look a bit peaky actually." He said with a note of concern. "And before you ask," he said, positioning himself like he was about to give me a lecture, "we didn't do anything; I am a gentleman Ells and shagging you whilst you're blotto isn't my style, okay?"

I immediately coloured up.

What was I thinking? Once again, I'd drunk myself vulnerable and flaked out in this lovely man's home. I felt very ashamed of myself.

As soon as I'd hydrated enough to stumble to the bathroom to freshen up, I resolved to return home as soon as possible.

The bathroom was surprisingly hygienic. Not what I was expecting from a bachelor pad.

I opened his bathroom cabinets hoping to find some deodorant and realised why, not only his bathroom, but the rest of his space revealed many feminine touches. Matching scatter cushions was the big giveaway. Single chaps rarely, if ever, have coordinated scatter cushions in the spaces.

He and Paula had clearly lived together, and a quick look through his bathroom cabinet confirmed my suspicions. Fake eyelashes, nail varnish remover, tampons!

I made myself presentable, used a hairbrush to sweep up my hair and tried to look far more groomed, as George re-appeared with some delicious, steaming black coffee,

"Here you go lovely, this'll help." He handed over the coffee and, at the same time, stroked my shoulder in a comradely way. I accepted it graciously, had a couple of sips, then went to grab my bag and head off with as much dignity as I could gather.

"Why did you let me drink so much George?" I asked quizzically.

"Because it was fun watching you loosen up a bit." He smirked.

"Loosen up?" I started to get defensive.

"Well, you've got a bit of the Ice Maiden about you. I enjoyed seeing you lark about!" He grinned.

I was NOT happy at all.

I was annoyed at myself and felt foolish that I'd been played.

Okay, no real harm done; just a bit tipsy with a work colleague, nothing had taken place, nothing I couldn't look the snotty Paula in the eyes with.

Time to go home and return to being the Ice Maiden. The comment struck me, and inside I felt a little jolt. Is that how the rest of my colleagues viewed me? A Miss Jean Brody type character, a slightly faded, past her prime joke?

I studiously avoided being in the staffroom for a couple of weeks in case I bumped into George or Paula and tried to carry on with my routines. I was starting to forget about the incident when I was alone rifling through some library resources at the School and got cornered by George, who came right up to me and said quietly,

"Ells, have you been avoiding me?"

"Yes, err, I have, I suppose. I was just embarrassed, sorry." I looked down at my hands on a textbook.

"Awww come on, it wasn't that bad; I'm sorry as well. I've had mates come round for all-nighters, just felt comfortable with you. It's nothing, honestly."

"Might be nothing to you George, but I felt like I let down my guard, I feel a bit foolish, and I don't want to tackle Paula over anything!"

"Paula? What's Paula got to do with anything?" His tone changed.

"You know, your live-in?"

"Paula's my Ex-Girlfriend, we NEVER lived together Ellie."

"Really? The flat's full of girlie crap...and CUSHIONS!" I seethed.

George looked at me really hard, then threw his head, took a step back and laughingly said, "Oh Crikey...No! That's my flat-shares girlfriend's stuff; she's over some weekends. Oh Ellie, good job you don't teach Maths putting two and two together making five, you Gonk!"

I immediately went red.

He moved forward, put the book I was holding on the shelf and kissed me, pushing me against the bookshelves hidden from the Staffroom. He pressed his body into mine until I could feel every inch of him. George kept kissing me until I had to ask him to stop in case anyone came into the space.

"Ellie, Ellie, Ellie, you temptress, you're so sexy. Every time you entered the Staffroom, I was aware of you, and you always smelt so good." He purred. "Let's go on a proper date, yeah?" He said once he'd extracted himself from me.

"Okay, can we go to the Kino? The one by Sasky Park?"

"When, when, when? God Woman, you're making me crazy" he whispered.

I just giggled and gave him my business card with my number on it.

"Text me, see you Friday outside Kino Sasky, 8pmish?"

With that, I gave him a brief peck on the cheek and left the building. I practically skipped home to my apartment. George was a catch. He was attractive, bright, and liked me!

I couldn't wait till 'kino night'. I have no memory of what we watched, George's hands were all over me, and I think we snogged throughout most of the film.

When I wasn't teaching, I was with George.

We kept it secret from everyone at the School, being careful to be discrete.

I've always hated work colleagues slobbering over each other when they get together; it's distracting! We often socialised with a group from the School, so we could go out and about, and no-one would make a comment about us being together. We had stolen moments of togetherness in the staffroom or library, or even an empty classroom. It did add a certain frisson to the working day, almost like having an affair.

He'd often swing over to my apartment so we had some privacy. He had to share his large apartment with a mate and his girlfriend, who did indeed stay over at weekends!

I knew it wouldn't lead anywhere.

George had made it clear he wasn't for settling down yet and wasn't looking for family.

He wasn't perfect, just perfectly fine for now!

George enjoyed showing me around the city he loved. We both had a shared love of music, cinema, and theatre. Warsaw was a dream of a place for high art and culture. What was seen as expensive and exclusive in London was unbelievably cheap in Warsaw. There was no way on a teacher's salary in the UK I could have afforded the amount of classical music, Avant-guard art exhibitions and theatre shows I was introduced to during my time over there.

One really memorable evening was watching a performance of Mozart's 'Requiem' performed at St. Jacek's, a beautiful Baroque-style church that had survived the WWII bombings and several invasions over the centuries.

It was the perfect backdrop for listening to sublime music by Warsaw Opera.

The acoustics were astounding. It only cost me about 27ZL, which was the equivalent of about £8 at the time. I felt very grateful to have experienced this performance; it really touched my soul. I think I was tearful throughout most of it. Could you imagine going to Covent Garden and listening to world-class opera for £8?

Life was more interesting with George, and for a month or so, as the weather got kinder, we enjoyed socialising and spending time with friends, appearing to all as 'just good pals' whilst secretly having a passionate fling.

So imagine my disappointment when Paula came back on the scene.

What is it about exes that make them appear like bad pennies, just turning up? I thought.

Even though George and I had been discrete at the School, our liaison had got back to Paula.

She was not best pleased and tackled me about it after a long day of teaching, when I'd returned one evening to go back to the School for some photocopying.

"Hey Ellie, can we have a chat?" She barked.

"I haven't got long Paula, I'm off home now." I replied wearily.

"Is it true about you and George?"

"What are you asking me Paula?" I met her gaze.

"Don't play dumb; you've been fucking him, haven't you?"

"Excuse me? It's none of your business Paula actually!"

"You do know we were on a break? He's still seeing me, you know. We've had a good chat and sorted some stuff out, so back off lady!" She practically spat in my face.

Shocked, I tried to steady my composure, "He told me you were over-possessive and wanted to settle down, which he told me he did not want." I snapped in retaliation.

"We met up last week; he's slept with me you know; he's missed me." She said cruelly. "I mean, how old are you? Forty or something? We are going to give it another go, sure, he doesn't want to settle for now, but he will, with me, EVENTUALLY!" She said wide-eyed, nose-flared.

Stunned, I just grabbed my bag and left. Tears welling up, but I didn't want her to see that. This was a classic menage a trois drama I was in the middle of. What a dupe!

Had I been walking around with a neon sign, 'Sad, Gullible, Middle-Aged Woman?'

When I returned to my apartment, I slammed the front door so hard in frustration it made a shudder, and the coat hook hanger fell off!

How dare they! How could George be so duplicitous?

All the victim thoughts crowded in, when the simple truth was that I'd allowed him to do this to me. I had been blindsided by my loneliness and grabbed the first available show of affection like a drowning woman reaching for a floating log, desperate to survive.

My pride had suffered a whack. I'm a genuinely decent, kind, thoughtful person, but Paula obviously deeply cared for George even though I thought she was an annoying chancer; in her eyes, I was the interloper, the opportunist.

I spent the rest of the evening in a haze, as I wandered around Saski Park. It had become my sanctuary and place of solace. A chance to ground myself and be surrounded with greenery and beautiful gardens.

Parc Saski had the Tomb of The Unknown Warrior by what remained of the Triple Arch of the Old Saxon Palace Colonnade. It was destroyed in 1945 and is constantly guarded by tall soldiers in national dress uniforms. It is always decorated with candles and flowers, so as I passed, I sighed and put my little domestic drama into context.

It had been a Royal Park, designed in the 1700s and had become Warsaw's first public park with some world-class garden statuary. Indeed, on a brief late spring visit with my daughter, we visited the park together. She had loved running in and out of the statues; for some reason, she would stop at the Baroque carving of the figure of 'Wisdom', telling me she liked that one the best because it 'looked a bit like Mummy reading!'.

So when I approached it, I started to sob and release my emotions.

I had been played by George. I was crying not because I was broken-hearted but because I was annoyed with myself. After my therapeutic stroll around the park, I resolved to tackle George about when he had planned to tell me about returning to his ex.

How was I going to handle seeing George and Paula together at the School again? Our paths would cross eventually, although thankfully not that often, as they both had separate teaching roles that kept them out of the city centre during the day at least. However, I would see them at the once-a-month team meeting at the School.

If I made a huge drama, it could be difficult within our shared friendship group of teaching colleagues. I resolved to be as dignified as I could be, quietly enraged and give them both a wide-berth whilst I licked my wounds.

Before I could think it through, I received a text message from George. Paula had obviously informed him that she'd told me to back off.

"Hi Ells, can you meet me for a drink? I'm guessing you think I'm an utter shit. Paula told you about us, that's not how I wanted this to go."

"Fine. See you in 10mins." I tapped back in reply.

As soon as I'd entered the bar, George stood up to meet me and attempted to pat my shoulder. I immediately slapped his hands down.

"Look Ells, I'm really sorry, didn't want to end it like this."

'Huh! Really George? You got Paula to do the dirty work!'

"It's complicated, Paula and I are complicated; we've got history; she got pregnant a few months ago, an accident and had a termination. I just freaked out, couldn't handle it. It messed us up." He gulped.

"I really like you Ells, but Paula is, persuasive, and I think she genuinely loves me. We've overlapped a bit, sorry, sorry." He said in a rush.

I sat down, lowered my voice with as much controlled rage as was physically possible and started,

"Firstly, you played me and overlapped; you slept with her last week, last week! You know what? I'm not heartbroken, I don't love you, it's just annoying and not fair! I whispered harshly.

"Secondly, I feel sorry for Paula, you know, you really should make up your mind about what you want in a relationship George and stop flip-flopping. And finally - you owe me a drink, you bastard! Okay, trot back to Paula, but don't even think about me, being a bit on the side; after this drink, I'm going, I'll not be troubling you again!"

Win some; you lose some.

I hadn't invested too much emotional intelligence in this liaison. Frankly, they deserved each other.

Over the past three months or so, I'd had some sexual healing, and it made me realise I was still attractive to men. Time to lick my wounds and enjoy socialising more, now the sun was shining, and clear azure skies were overhead again.

CHAPTER 12

The Korma Incident

Apart from Paula giving me the evil eye a couple of times at the School, and George and I having hurried changes of direction when we spotted each other, it all settled down after a few weeks. Then, I bumped into Paula in the School Canteen one lunchtime. I deliberately went up to her and said,

"Look Paula, I'm sorry about everything."

"S'okay, I know you and George were just a fling, whilst he was on a break from me. He knows what he was missing, we're all good now, but thanks for the apology; I thought you would eventually."

She tossed her golden hair imperiously and grabbed her food tray.

Ouch! Any sympathy I might have felt for her evaporated immediately. Honestly, they deserved each other; I'd had a lucky escape and I resolved right there and then to get my own back.

Now some of you reading this might feel that I should have just been magnanimous; I, on the other hand, felt a sense of relief.

My revenge plan was formulating in my head; how dare they both play me to leverage the power-play in their relationship?

I was going to get them back, but in a subtle way. Now that Paula felt she'd got the moral high ground, and I didn't actively avoid seeing them when I went out in mixed company with our shared friendship circle, no-one other than us three knew what the dynamic was. George and I had never flirted in front of our colleagues, and to give them their due, neither George nor Paula said a word in front of others.

It made the execution of my plan so much easier. I resolved to give a curry party at my tiny apartment in the city. I'd had a practice run weeks earlier with an egg and chips party for my ex-pat friends; they'd travel for miles for home-cooked comforts.

It was my practice run for the big denouement.

George and Paula came with about ten or twelve colleagues. Lots of fried eggs and buckets of chips later, vodka, music, smoking, and laughter, we were all full of 'bonhomie' and terribly 'grown up' about it all. Ha!

I have a deep well of vengeance I can draw upon when I'm crossed.

When someone is considered a friendly soul, they can get away with evil deeds unnoticed and more convincingly. My plan was simple revenge.

The Bard said, 'Revenge is a dish best served cold'; I say 'Revenge is a dish best served Korma'.

George and Paula were going to be unsuspecting after I'd broken the ice at the egg and chip party. That was exactly how I wanted it to play out.

Only I would know of my Pyrrhic victory, only I would gain any sense of revenge and retribution, and in a sense, only I would have to take responsibility for my actions. The date was set, text messages sent back and forth, reminders sent, and dates put in diaries. The trap was set.

The evening of the curry party arrived.

The word had spread amongst the ex-pat community, so on the evening itself, I had a few extra guests. My cute but tiny apartment was rammed. There was a lot of chatter, music, beer, and vodka drunk. The atmosphere was really chilled.

Many of the guests had drawn back the floor-to-ceiling net drapes to look at the amazing Warsaw skyline and the Palace of Culture & Science lit up like a wedding cake.

In the '90s, you could see for miles on a clear night; it looks very different today as many more tall skyscrapers have ringed the Palace to obscure its dominance on the horizon. So everyone was standing up, craning their necks, trying to observe the city landmarks.

The smell of my homemade Beef Korma was wafting through the room from the kitchen.

I'd tracked down the Indian spices to an out-of-the-way Indian food store. Indian restaurants were definitely classed as 'exotica' at the time, but what Brit can resist a 'Ruby Murray'? I'd managed to buy some poppadums and pickles and made some raita sauce with yoghurt and cucumber. It all looked very authentic.

When eventually everyone sat down at my extended table or on laps seated with trays, it went silent as I ladled the delicious meal individually onto plates from the kitchen.

Logistically, I could not have served to table, and the plan wouldn't have worked.

Everyone enjoyed the meal; we could have been in Birmingham at a Balti Restaurant; it seemed like home. Lots of conversations even with the despicable pair, George and Paula.

Paula asked, "What's the recipe?"

"If I told you, I'd have to kill you! Ha, Ha, Ha!" (everyone laughed)

George said, "Didn't know you were such a great cook, Ells".

Finally, folks started to clear off once the meal and a couple of rounds of coffee and drinks had been had.

It had been a delicious success.

As I collected all the dishes and loaded the dishwasher, I poured myself a glass of red wine and toasted myself that, as far as George and Paula were concerned, they'd eaten exactly the same Beef Korma as the other guests.

If only they could have seen me as I washed out the dog food cans I'd hidden under the sink to place in the rubbish-bin.

I'd cooked their dish separately, with the same sauce as the others. I had to serve it in the kitchen as I didn't want them to see it was in a separate serving dish.

I'd nearly wet my pants when Paula had gone on and on about how tender it was; she clearly wanted to replicate it to impress George, as she didn't really appreciate George enjoying my cooking!

"Just ask for a choice cut of beef at the butcher's." I'd told her.

The irony was the brand name on the can of dog food was 'Choice Cuts'.

I really hoped they didn't have any ill-effects, but I have to confess, visions of them puking up or running to the toilet really cheered me up.

The following Monday at School, they both came up to me saying it was the best curry they'd had for ages and glad we were all 'friends' again.

No Shit Sherlock, I thought.

CHAPTER 13

Serendipity

Marzena took it upon herself to make sure she had a fellow comrade-in-arms. We both were single and had a child.

Poland is an overwhelmingly Catholic country. Marzena was a Catholic, but much to her mother's disgust, non-practicing and divorced. At the time, it was pretty brave for a single woman with a child to live so independently. However, times and conservative attitudes were changing rapidly.

I enjoyed her company too, although I suspected part of my appeal was to appease her mother, who thought I was a 'sensible English friend' and had clearance as a chaperone rather than her male teaching colleagues.

Polish pubs were raucous places.

A mixture of a classic British pub atmosphere but with extensive barbecue facilities, usually outside in a courtyard. Who doesn't like a Kielbasa sausage with their beer?

One Friday after work, Marzena announced she was meeting up with the 'crowd' at Pod Barylka - a really cosy pub renowned for its extensive beer and sausage offerings.

Since the 1990s, Polish beers such as Zywiec (probably the most historic brand) and Okocim have developed into well-known brands in the UK.

Pod Barylka was pretty central in the city and had established itself as a monthly outdoor gathering of the teachers from the School. A live-music event consisting of some really talented jazz musicians was entertaining the crowd, and the barbecue was already fired up.

It was situated in the middle of a large, cobbled courtyard under a round sort of hut. The fire was fed by logs under a huge round tray with rows and rows of grills covered in Kielbasa sausages constantly rolled back and forth by attendants.

The smell was so inviting. It was all designed to make you salivate, make you thirsty and guzzle glasses of beer. Obviously, there were spirits available, but the beer was cheap and plentiful.

Most of our group stood around in an expanding circle by several upturned wooden barrels. They made the perfect height for tables to rest the glasses on.

The senses were heightened, by the salty tang of sizzling and dripping sausages, counteracted by the sweet-smelling blooms in large planters, dotted around to break up the space. The courtyard looked magical in the twilight, with twinkling outdoor lights.

After the first couple of rounds of gossiping about the School owners, we started settling down to the serious business of eating and drinking.

I peeled off to sit down at a bench to eat my sausage away from the group in peace. I was happy with my own company and just sat soaking up the heady smells and atmosphere.

I did feel like the 'mum' of the group sometimes, but I could hold my own socially and quickly established myself with the moniker of 'Funny Ellie' so, in this state of reverie, I didn't notice Marzena come up behind me and tap me on the shoulder. It made me jump, and I dropped the last morsel of my sausage.

"Marzena! You silly cow, don't do that; you'll give me a heart attack!" I laughed.

"Aww Sorry Pana Ella!" She giggled, "Can I introduce you to Lisa?" She pushed the woman hanging back towards me.

"Hi Ellie! I'm Lisa." She said whilst shaking my hand, 'Heard you're British?' She smiled, revealing perfectly even white teeth and a Boston twang to her accent.

"Oh Hello! You're American; is that a Boston accent?" I shouted over the music that had started up.

"Yeah! Well, I'm based in Washington now, but I was raised in Mass'. I'm over in the city with another school, teaching for a few months. Just wanted to get over to Europe. I'm staying in Praga."

"Oh, poor you," I said without stopping myself; the beer had loosened my tongue.

Praga was a Soviet-drab, grey and depressing housing project. I'd never visited, but you could see it looking across the bridge.

"Don't I know it!" Giggled Lisa. "Yeah, it's a little rough, but housing is a lot cheaper that side of the river; I've got more money for travelling and visiting cool places in Poland!" I liked her bright, sunny demeanour immediately.

Over several beers and a couple more sausages, she was firmly ensconced into our tribe.

About an hour into the noisy storytelling, gossipy intrigues about our shared teaching experiences and bosses, Lisa casually mentioned her brother, Lucas was 'in town' also teaching at another Language School closer to me on the 'posh' side of the city.

I didn't think much about that remark until another ten minutes or so later, when I turned my head to chat to Marzena and there, sitting next to me, was a really attractive man!

I was taken aback; he did a sort of wave and said, "Hi, I'm Lucas!" Shooting a look at Lisa. "The clever one!"

To which Lisa guffawed and replied, "Oh yeah, Bro?"

We all laughed.

Marzena's 'man radar' was immediately switched on, and her eyebrows shot up as if to say, 'Oh, Hello?'.

She immediately started to flirt with him. It was hilarious; the eye-fluttering, hair tossing, stretching her endless tanned legs, and laughing at everything Lucas said. Lucas was really entertaining; he had a soft, deep American accent and a very dry sense of humour. The following hour flew by.

Eventually, I started to look at my watch; I didn't have anything planned for the weekend, but it was gone 11 pm, and I knew it would take at least thirty minutes to return home. The last trams were about midnight, but I didn't like travelling alone on the Metro very late at night. Most females can understand the inherent unease and vulnerability of travelling on your own late at night. Lucas clocked me checking my watch.

"Have you got to go soon?" He enquired, giving me a full clear look from unbelievably blue eyes.

I gulped. He was drop-dead gorgeous. Properly handsome, clean-shaven skin, rich brown, soft curls with silver flecks at his temples which bobbed when his head moved, and long, dark, thick eyelashes framing dazzlingly clear blue eyes.

Don't blush, don't blush, don't blush!

Blushing, I said. "Well, it's getting a little late for the Metro. I don't like travelling on it on my own this time of night."

"Hey! Would you like me to escort you home?

I don't believe we live so far apart; you're near Plac Bancowy, right?" He flashed the same bright smile as Lisa, same perfect teeth.

Oh God! That smile, those eyes! Don't blush! I couldn't have signalled that I fancied Lucas more clearly if I'd had a flashing neon sign on my head!

"How did you know I lived near Plac Bankovy?"

"Marzena told Lisa." He confessed.

"Oh no, no, no, you stay with your sister and catch up, and I came here with Marzena." I said graciously.

"Ha! I see Lisa every week; I really don't mind Ellie. I'll escort both of you if she's ready to go. Lisa is staying with friends this weekend; she won't be travelling alone."

Marzena's eyebrows raised; she quickly assessed the situation and waved her hand, "Hey Ella, I'm fine, I'll go home with the others; we are going onto a club - the night is young!" She started gyrating in her seat.

I just laughed; she winked at me as if to say, 'The coast is clear, go for it!' I was relieved I didn't have her competition.

Lucas said something about settling his bar bill and to meet him by the entrance to the pub.

Lisa smiled and leaned over in my direction as I was gathering my bag. "Lucas must like you, he rarely stays long when we go out, and he asked Marzena where you lived!" She giggled.

"Well, it was lovely meeting you, hopefully our paths will cross soon; we could go for a coffee or something?" I shook her hand to signal my going.

"Sure, likewise, See you soon Ellie!" She smiled, then turned to chat to other friends.

I went to settle my bill and pop to the ladies, and by the time I'd returned, I could see Lucas waiting by the door, all 6ft 2in of male gorgeousness.

"Oh hi Ellie, is Marzena coming too?" He enquired, looking over my head back to our crowd.

"No, she wants to go out clubbing with her other friends, oh to be twenty-something again, all that energy, eh?" I giggled.

"Gawd, nope, my clubbing days are over; this is a late night for me; I'm the old man on my team!" He smiled

"Old man? Hardly! Thank you Lucas." I smiled as he held the door open to let me through.

"Oh call me Luc, only Mom calls me Lucas, usually when she's pissed off at me! Yeah, they're all gap-year youngsters where I work. I'm mid-30s, ancient!" He laughed and glanced sideways at me.

"Well, we're about the same age, snap!"

We chatted amiably as we hopped onto the tram, swapping stories of why we'd gone out to Poland.

I found out he was doing some post-graduate research into WWII and was out on secondment for a year from a College near his home in Massachusetts.

"How's your Polish language skills coming along, Ellie?" He suddenly changed the conversation.

"Well, rubbish, haven't got past basic, survival language." I laughed.

"Shocking! You Brits are such lazy, language learners." He mocked.

He then started showing off, by chatting to a passenger on the tram. I watched him chatting animatedly, his handsome face lighting up when he'd made himself understood.

I started to zone out, my mind drifting off, imagining what it would be like to kiss this gorgeous man!

Shocked, I snapped out of it to realise that my stop was rapidly approaching opposite the Park.

"Oh, nice area Ellie. Did you know the 'Tomb of The Unknown Warrior' is based in this park?" He said authoritatively.

"Yes, it's been an eye-opener to me how much they're never allowed to forget about the war in this city." I said.

"Aww don't get me started, I've got so many stories I'm writing up for my research- it's a well-ploughed subject, WWII stories!" He smirked.

"I bet you do Luc (mocking tone) Oh, come up and listen to my WWII stories; yeah, I bet that impresses the ladiezzzz." I flirted.

Luc, wide-eyed, bowed his head towards mine, and I got a whiff of his fresh aftershave. "A gentleman never tells!" He whispered.

I play-slapped his arm good-naturedly. It was like an electric shock going through both of us at the same time. Luc raised his eyebrows and smirked at me.

The tram pinged for the stop; he glanced out of the window, grabbed my hand, led me off the tram, and ran across the road to the park opposite my apartment.

To this day, I've no idea why we ran to the park. I suppose I had an inkling he liked me. At the nearest tree, he stopped abruptly, pulled me to him and said,

"Come here, You English Rose!" Then he kissed me passionately, my lips, my face, my neck. He was very ardent, and time was suspended. The feel of his lips was firm, but tender; he kept moaning and kissing, kissing, kissing. It was wonderful.

"Damn Ellie, I've wanted to do that all night!" He whispered.

"Really? I thought you'd go for Marzena." I sighed.

"Marzena? No way! She's got that look of a man-eater. Too much for me, that one; she's too young and flighty, my dear!" He nuzzled into my neck.

We kissed for ages, then I felt very sleepy and realised it was nearing midnight.

"Luc, I'd better go, and before you ask." I broke away from him, looked into those deep pools and said. "And before you ask, you're not stopping over, okay? The last tram is in a few minutes!"

"Understood, m'lady - but damn girl, you're so lovely, I want to see you again; you have to say yes! Say yes, Ellie!" He implored.

"I'll text you my number; give me your phone, quick, before your tram comes!"

Numbers swapped, I reluctantly drew away from his warm, manly shoulders and male scent. He texted me immediately, after he got onto his tram when I was at my apartment door. I was shattered but wired. It took me ages to finally drop off to sleep.

At 7am, my phone pinged with a text message:
"Couldn't sleep. Your fault, you gorgeous english rose. Lunch? Choose somewhere and text me. See you later? Xx"

Two Kisses! This was so unexpected. I had planned to ease back into dating after the 'Korma' incident.

I smiled and compared how my life was opening up to possibilities after only three or four months. Arriving in winter at Warsaw Coach Station alone, sad, anxious, drinking herbata and wondering what the hell I'd decided to do with my life!

I settled back in my bed, and a huge smile spread over my face.

I wouldn't have met someone like Lucas back home. Why did I have to be separated from my baby girl and have to travel thousands of miles to find someone like him?

Time for some fun Ellie!

CHAPTER 14

Exploration

I've always considered Warsaw Old Town a very romantic place.

Little alleys and cobbled streets; an ideal city to explore on foot, as major attractions are relatively close together.

However, I remember ruining several pairs of high-heeled shoes and boots in the early days on uneven pavements.

I decided to wear flat, clumpy, thick-soled shoes that many Warsovian women wore walking about. It was definitely a case of comfort over style, but they saved a crumpled ankle. It allowed me to walk miles across the city and down to the mighty River Vistula viewing some real architectural gems.

A lovely Warsaw legend is a tale of a Mermaid who lived in the Vistula and protected the city by singing songs to the people. There were statues of the mermaid all over the city.

Lucas had started to become my 'Gentleman caller'. The first few dates were just walking to various attractions, having lunch, visiting the kino, a couple of delicious dinners in authentic Polish bistros, and visiting parks and museums.

Just more opportunities for Luc to show off his rapidly developing language skills.

I wanted to go slow on the dating side of things; we were attracted to each other, but I didn't want to just bed-hop for sex. The experiences with Bogdan and George were enough for me to want to take my time with Luc.

The inevitable happened though, in the most unromantic of circumstances.

Luc called around unannounced one afternoon, two or three weeks into us dating.

It was a little embarrassing at the time; I was looking like a hot mess as I was in the middle of dying my hair!

The doorbell to my apartment rang; thinking it was a delivery or my neighbours, I quickly wrapped a towel turban around my head, shoved on a silky dressing gown and grabbed open the door.

I stood wide-eyed, mouth gaping, and immediately blushing as red as my hair dye. Luc was leaning on the door frame, wearing a tweed jacket, chinos, and a blue open-collared shirt, and carrying what looked like a roughly picked bunch of flowers in his hand. His smile was wide and brilliant on his smooth face.

We looked at one another for a second or two in shock. Eyebrows raised, and then I felt a trickle of fresh hair dye drip into my eye.

Luc grinned, "Lordy! There's me thinking it was all natural, you're busted my girl!" Roaring with laughter, he leaned forward and kissed me hard. His lips were very sweet.

"I can't stop thinking about you woman; got it bad Ells, just want to be with you." He said, pushing me into my kitchen, dumping the weedy flowers into my sink and grabbing my dressing gown tie.

"Er, what do you think you're up to Mr?" I laughingly chided, knowing full well he was a man on a mission.

"I'm just lovin' unwrapping the goodies here." He started swaying to some soul music that was playing on my radio whilst expertly sliding off my gown and caressing my freshly washed skin.

We spent a long time just caressing, swaying and kissing. The man was delicious, and I wanted to take my time, but I felt my resistance crumbling. The towel turban stained with the red evidence tumbled onto the floor. Suddenly there was more urgency, and I felt him press into me.

"Darlin', you are driving me mad!"

What was a girl to do?

When we finally surfaced hours later, the flowers had wilted in the sink, and the apartment was pitch black.

Luc grabbed me as I went to the kitchen for a drink of water and smothered me with many, many kisses. His trim, lithe, athletic body spooned into mine, and he wrapped his manly arms around me. We both stood completely naked, looking out across the amazingly twinkly, Warsaw skyline in quiet sanctuary with each other.

We had found each other, both fish out of water, both escaping our lives, in our own countries to a certain extent.

We knew it was going to be a journey of discovery. The exciting first steps when even a night vista took on a panoramic, light show more vivid than a fireworks display. When we were together, lights burned brighter, the air was sweeter, food more nourishing. Life surged through us. We were rehabilitated in that quiet moment of stillness; we were incandescent and lit from within.

Time slowed down for our 'lost weekend'. After days in bed, sending out for pizza, I insisted I needed a break and fresh air!

"There's too much of a good thing y'know darling." I sighed when he pulled a face at my suggestion of going on a walk.

Luc then lit up and said, "Hey!... Let's walk the 'Royal Route' in the city".

The Royal Route (Tract Krolewski) is a very attractive route which runs from the Castle Square (Plac Zamkowy) along the left bank of the River Vistula, between major thoroughfares of Krakowskie Prezdmiescie and Nowy Swiat.

This area developed from the Middle Ages and, over the centuries, amassed many churches and palaces, which attracted Warsaw's wealthiest citizens to settle.

We set off, and Luc must have kissed me a hundred times as we ambled along, together with a running commentary of his immense knowledge of Warsaw.

I learnt very early on that WWII was his passionate subject, but he made the city come alive to me through his eyes. I could listen to him for hours. He was a natural teacher. He dragged me along for another couple of hours, then to his favourite destination, the Polish Military Museum, where many vehicles were exhibited from the war.

This set up a pattern of walks around the city; they all somehow had something of interest for Luc to study!

We quickly fell into a routine of travelling all over the city on trams, exploring nooks and alleys away from the tourist trails, always snuggled close, breathing each other's air like lovers do. Swaying together, holding each other tight as the tram shuddered.

We were just happy to be in each other's orbit.

It was now early summer in Warsaw and stifling hot and humid. I was taken by surprise at how wet and sticky the city had become.

My hair suffered and was permanently curly and frizzy. I wore it much longer in those days and so mostly resorted to wearing it up and away from my face.

Luc would always take great delight in undoing my hair and letting it loose. He would constantly twirl and twist it in his fingers when we sat quietly watching TV or reading in each other's apartments. A constant touch. He was the most tactile man I'd ever dated. It felt like my hair was a tie between us, we were tied metaphorically, and it was incredibly soothing.

On one of our Sunday afternoon trips to Wilanow Palace, a beautiful grand family palace built in the late 1600s for King Jan 111 Sobieski, set in a grand Baroque Park under the stunning Chinese gazebo, Luc whispered into my ear,

"I've fallen for you Ells, I love you…I mean it. I know it's not just you; you're a two-for-one deal here."

I just held him very close. I wanted to say it back, but I just had to process this without making him feel vulnerable.

"I know, this feels different; I'm certainly falling for you too Luc."

We were swept up in a romantic bubble as we travelled home on the tram. As we stepped off by my apartment opposite Saski Park, the heavens opened violently. A very sharp, heavy, drenching downpour!

Instead of sensibly running into the apartment block for shelter, Luc grabbed my hand and ran to a stone monument, by the park entrance ,kissing me passionately.

We were completely drenched in warm rain, like standing fully clothed in a shower. We were totally oblivious to anything.

Time stood still.

We declared our love for each other. I could feel the dampness from the rain soaking onto my skin; Luc held me fast, kissing my face and saturated hair, nuzzling my neck, wet skin-on-skin feeling him press so hard against the granite stone. It was a mad thing to do and wonderful. My skin was wet and on fire at the same time.

I'd never felt like that before.

Standing entwined, dripping, caressing and not caring if anyone saw us, was the most deliciously, erotic episode of my life to that point.

CHAPTER 15

Rose-Tinted Romance

Life continued apace over the early summer. We were busy teaching at our respective Language Schools. Luc was continuing with his research and socialising with his sister Lisa, whom I was getting to know better as well.

Lisa would sometimes drop in if she had a teaching assignment in this district; we'd have a coffee at the little cafe under my apartment block and just chit-chat.

She'd often tell me stories of Luc as a kid and spill the beans on some of his relationship choices that she didn't approve of. We were friendly and comradely. I thought, she'll be a family ally.

I liked her very much, and we became buddies. She was interested in politics and worked as an intern in Washington DC. She was an aide to a Senator and got to know the behind-the-scenes machinations of Washington, the State Capitol.

Lisa had wanted to visit Europe to widen her knowledge of the world and to take some time out of the bipartisan hothouse atmosphere of American politics.

We would socialise with teachers from each other's schools, so our circle of ex-pats became wider and wider. Visiting cafes, cukerinias (cake shops) and kino's, our social diaries were full.

Luc and I had become exclusive for a couple of months when I broached the subject of my daughter's impending school holiday visit to Warsaw.

I'd been missing her terribly and had been saving hard to pay for her airfare. We had spoken about the arrangements over the phone.

As luck would have it, some friends of my ex-husband and I were visiting Poland, Krakow, for a holiday. They agreed to chaperone my daughter for the outbound flight from Heathrow and stop over at Warsaw before catching a connecting flight to Krakow. It was incredibly generous of them.

Luc had understood from the day he met me I was a mother. My circumstances were unusual; I was dating like a single person, my parental duties temporarily on hold…but I was still a mother. Luc had never married or had children.

Our relationship was maturing rapidly, hot-housed in the humid conditions of a summer in Warsaw. Two ex-pats living a sort of extended holiday romance. This upcoming trip was a test set by me, I suppose, about how he interacted with Rebecca.

One day at the Language School, my friend Marzena asked me what Luc's horoscope sign was. When I said Capricorn, she pulled a face, "Oh (pause) Be careful with him; he's a homeboy." She said matter-of-factly.

"Pardon? He's overseas Marzena!" I laughed.

"Seriously, Ella, he's very close to his mama, be careful!" She warned.

I was a little taken aback. She knew how happy and cheerful I'd been over the past few weeks.

Work was progressing well; I was feeling more confident about exploring the city; I was making friends and tentative plans to place my daughter in an Anglo-American school in the city, and to develop a life for us to settle down into. I'd met a marvellous chap who professed his love and affection, which was the cherry on the top.

This suddenly, felt like a small weed creeping into my perfect garden. I didn't like it.

"Really? I thought you liked Lucas? In fact, I remember you flirted with him!" I snapped.

"No, sure, he's cute, but I'm your friend Pana Ella, just slow down; it's getting pretty serious, no?" Her tone was questioning.

"Honestly Marzena, I'm fine; we're both grown-ups and know what we want in life. How could you possibly know he's a 'mummy's boy'?" I said as I turned to make myself busy and end this conversation.

I didn't appreciate her raining-on-my-parade.

It was a very definite opinion on her part that I didn't ask for. That was Marzena, she was just black and white with her opinions, no shades of grey. The woman was talented, beautiful but very wrong about Luc!

Later that evening, Luc called to catch up on my day. He was staying in his own apartment for a few days as he was snowed under with research writing.

I'd been brooding over Marzena's remarks all evening. It was uncomfortable. I felt like a bucket of cold water had been hurled over my lovely 'bubble'. After all, what did I really know of Luc's life back in the US? I thought.

Luc picked up on my mood early into our conversation,

"What's up hun? You sound a bit flat tonight?" He questioned.

"Oh yeah, just missing Rebecca (slight pause) …I just want her trip to be happy, and I'm feeling a little stressed about how you two might get on… (another pause). Do you miss your family back home Luc?" I tried to keep it light.

"Well, y'know I love it over here; it's so different from back home in Mass. I don't feel anything can touch me here, like in a bubble." He sounded wary.

"So, what about your family? Apart from Lisa, I've never heard you talk about them, your other brothers, you know?"

"Ohhh, serious talk tonight, huh? Well, my Mom has a large horse farm in Mass, near to Boston on the border of Connecticut…the family has another holiday home up in Vermont and another horse farm in Connect. The brothers are scattered all over; Phil's in New York, he's a big-cheese with an international insurance company (yawn) and Micky, he's in the Military, New Mexico; we don't see a lot of each other, to be honest. I moved in with Mom after my last relationship went bust out in California; I told you that. I went home to help Mom out a bit with the farm as she's getting on and to help me out to start again." He rattled on.

"So, you live with your Mum?" My tone came out accusatory.

"Whoa! Is that a crime now Ells?" He snapped.

"Oh no, no, no…silly, I'm just asking?" I said lightly, not wanting the rising panic to betray in my voice.

Marzena was right!

He lived with his mum in the US. A grown man. Why did this disappoint me? It was ridiculous, shallow, and annoyed me intensely that Marzena's instincts seemed better attuned than mine!

"I'm coming over, think you need a hug honey. I'll be over in 20, okay Ells?" He said urgently.

I think he felt like a can of worms had been opened, and he didn't want me brooding on the conversation overnight. True to his word, twenty minutes or so, my doorbell rang. I opened the door to see Luc holding the door frame with one hand, slightly bent over and wheezing.

"I've …just…er…ran…. awww come here honey!" He panted and launched himself at me with a huge bearhug. I was literally wrapped up in his arms and in bed within seconds.

End of conversation for now!

We spent most of the following morning before I had to go to work, clearing the air and opening up about our fears and foibles. It felt like we were much closer intellectually and emotionally.

I was calmer and excited to be with this man again. We made little plans about what we would do when my daughter came to visit. Lucas did want to get to know her too; he was very nervous as he hadn't had children in any of his previous relationships.

He did understand that I'd wanted to dig into his past if I was going to allow him to get closer to my daughter.

CHAPTER 16

Polish Tooth Fairy

I met Rebecca with her friendly chaperones at Okencie International Airport. It's Warsaw's only International airport and is relatively close to the city, being about four miles away.

There was only one terminal to navigate, so I waited patiently but fidgeting with nervous energy for the LOT (Polish State Airline) 747 flight to land from London Heathrow with its precious cargo.

I saw her little hazel-coloured bob and pink backpack before I noticed my friends; she caught my eye and broke free of them, running full tilt towards me, crying with her little arms outstretched. Tears of joy ran down our faces as she clung to me so tightly for a few seconds. I swear she had grown, and I smothered her perfect little face with kisses.

"Mummy, Mummy, My Mummy!" She wept.

"Precious darling, Mummy's missed you so much sweetheart!" I said, lifting her up for a massive hug.

We were oblivious to my friends, who were visibly moved at our reunion and had hung back for a few seconds to give us some privacy.

I thanked them profusely, but they didn't hang around too long as they had an interconnecting flight to Krakow to catch.

Rebecca and I clung to one another and giggled and chatted all the way back to my apartment on the tram. The tramway and the system of punching tickets fascinated her; of course, being a feisty, clever, independent seven-year-old, she had to have a go at punching the tickets herself.

"Let me do it Mummy! I can do it!" She asserted.

She then showed me a loose baby-tooth she was constantly wiggling that was soon to be released.

"Mum, Nanny and Grandad said the tooth-fairy would know how to find me in Poland," all wide-eyed and innocent.

"So, what's the going rate for baby-teeth these days?" I enquired.

"Well, I got 50p for the first tooth, but Grandad said that was a bit mean of Nanny, so swapped it for a whole pound coin Mummy!" She said in awe of her Grandads generosity.

Hmmm, I thought, better work out the Zloty tooth-fairy exchange rate.

Her back-molar was going to fall out imminently. Sure enough, the first evening, as she was preparing for bed, her constant wiggling produced the desired result. A cash-producing, bloody trophy!

We had the pantomime of where to place the tooth, "so the fairy has a chance to find it out here Mummy!"

I really should have forward planned the tooth extraction strategy a little better, as I found to my horror, that I had very little change left in the apartment.

I generally paid for things in dollars. I only had bits and pieces of shrapnel in coinage. I scraped together what I could find and hoped my clever young daughter wouldn't work out the exchange rate and think Polish tooth-fairies were a bit tight-fisted.

As soon as she was asleep, I sat gazing at her perfect angelic face for many minutes, feeling so grateful to be with her. I was suddenly very homesick. A wave of deep emotion poured out of me.

What sort of mother leaves her daughter with her parents for months on end to travel thousands of miles away to Eastern Europe? To 'find myself'; what did that even mean anymore?

Suddenly, my relationship with Lucas was brought into sharp focus. I really didn't want her to go back to my parents and the UK. However, I was contracted until September with the Language School, plus it wouldn't have been fair on my parents, who'd given me this breathing space. She was settled, spoilt to death by Mum and Dad, her doting Grandparents, and she still saw her Dad every two weeks, as regular as clockwork.

My self-indulgent weep lasted a few minutes. I felt immediately split in two, but I had to pull myself together and sort out the sodding tooth-fairy racket.

I nearly woke her up trying to gather all the coinage under her pillow and stop it rolling into the bedding. Mission accomplished, I turned in blissfully unaware my daughter had indeed woken up and was counting her haul of coins deposited by a seemingly generous foreign tooth-fairy.

The following day she accompanied me to the Language School, where I popped in to hand in some timesheets and do an hour's lesson preparation.

As luck would have it, Agnieska was strutting around the reception area with the secretaries. She immediately went to Rebecca and said, "Oh what a darling child! How could you leave her Pana Ella?"

I mumbled something and scooted her out of there as quickly as I could. I really didn't need her barbed judgement.

I felt my eyes moisten and throat tighten and tried to quickly gain my composure as I said to Rebecca, "We're going to meet my boyfriend at a new McDonalds in the city, would you like a Polish 'Happy Meal' darling?"

The first McDonald's restaurant opened at about the same time I went over to Warsaw. It was an exciting moment for most Warsovians, who felt they finally had some of the Western trappings.

It was quite expensive, so basically, only the middle-classes craved it initially. It was an instant hit when it opened, with queues around the city blocks for weeks.

We met Lucas outside the gleaming, shiny, new Mcdonald's towards the back end of Saski Park (Ogrod Saski). Luc seemed understandably nervous, but he soon had Rebecca engaged in animated conversation and looking for Polish tooth-fairy activity.

"So young lady, what did the tooth-fairy leave under your pillow? Can you treat me to a burger?" Luc said, laughing as he handed out the prized 'Happy Meal'.

"Oh just some coins; I think the tooth-fairy doesn't understand pounds in Poland." She smirked and looked slyly at me.

Luc's eyebrows raised conspiratorially as he lowered his head and said, "Do you think it was actually your Mom?"

A moment's silence. I was about to tell Luc to wind his neck in and to stop going on about the tooth-fairy's failings when Rebecca burst out laughing!

"I knew it was you Mum; I counted the change, which by my calculation, is pants really!"

Luc roared his head off and nodded sagely, "Well Rebecca, we'll have to see if we can't round that paltry sum up for you". He turned out his pockets for more coins.

"I like Luc Mum, he pays more than you do." She giggled.

We were all getting on splendidly after Luc bribed his way into my Rebecca's affections. Round One to the tooth-fairy and the American!

The long weekend flew by, with trips to the parks, kino, visits to cake shops, and picnics in Lazienki Park (Lazienki Krolewskie). Lazienki was another Royal park. Lazienki means bath. It had a bathing pavilion and now hosts the Chopin International Piano Concert every four years. A Chopin monument sculpted in 1908 is positioned by the side of a beautiful lake. Rebecca loved clambering all over the monuments, especially the great bronze Lions guarding the entrance.

Luc and her larked about, running, throwing ball games, and I could hear her chattering animatedly as he read her some story on her last evening with us.

My heart sank as I settled her down for the night. She started to cry and cling to me. "I don't want to go back home, please Mummy, let me stay; why can't I stay?" She wailed.

It broke my heart. I gently told her that I'd be home in two or three months, then we would decide if she wanted to come and live with Mummy all the time.

"I do Mum, I do like it here. Please Mum, I'll be good. Please." She pleaded.

In exhaustion, she finally dropped off, and as I kissed her goodnight, I felt utterly torn.

I had to make some fundamental life-changing decisions very soon. I couldn't go on drifting, running away in a 'bubble'. However necessary I had thought it was for my mental health a few months previously, the landscape of my life was changing rapidly.

Luc gave me a long hug; he didn't really say much to me; he could instinctively feel that the parting and farewells at the airport in the morning were going to be harrowing.

"Awww Ellie, she's a doll. What a great kid, and she's so smart. She had you, tooth-fairy Momma!" He said, trying to lighten my mood.

"Look, tomorrow's gonna be rough; I'll come with you both?" He said, trying to be supportive.

I just laid my head on his shoulder and wished life wasn't so complicated. To be honest, I think I cried myself to sleep in Luc's arms. He just supported me and tried to make life more bearable. I honestly don't know how we returned to Okencie airport in the morning.

I do remember gripping the barrier when the BA flight attendant chaperone approached us with a clipboard and called Rebecca's name. She shot a look of panic up at my face.

'It's all right darling; this lovely lady is going to sit with you and fly home with you till Nanny and Granddad collect you from Heathrow at the other end; she'll be with you all the time." Cue big sobs on both our parts, kissing and hugs, clinging onto one another.

Luc rubbed both of our backs in helpless camaraderie to try and soothe the parting.

The BA flight attendant said gently to Rebecca, "Hey Rebecca, my name's Alison. I promised your Mum I'll be with you all the time until your Grandparents collect you. I've got a special case for you for the trip. Would you like to see inside what I've packed for you?" She said, holding out a kiddie carry-on case.

She was clearly professionally trained, in the distraction techniques needed to prize wailing kids off their parents and onto planes.

Rebecca's head swivelled around; her curiosity caught her off-guard. She sniffled and lifted the cute backpack. The second the bag was taken, the flight attendant grabbed her hand and gently started to move away.

I'll never forget the mournful look on Rebecca's sad face as she took one last look behind her.

As soon as she was out of sight, I let out a heart-wrenching sob. I think it shocked Luc a little, and he stood there helplessly rubbing my back and shushing me, "Oh Ells, she'll be just fine; it'll be an adventure for her. Anyone can see you're a good Mom…I can…shhhhhh…shhhhh…honey."

"She'll feel like I don't want her…but I do! I DO! I think I need to go HOME'" I wailed.

Finally, Luc walked me out of the concourse and treated me to a Zurbrovka at our favourite bar, to numb the emotional pain. I was sad for days. However, a phone call home later in the week confirmed that she'd arrived tired and fractious, but after a good rest and some spoiling by her Granddad, who took her to the seaside for a treat, she was back to her bubbly self.

My Mum had assured me that Rebecca was impressed by Mum's boyfriend, especially that he was American and he really liked burgers, which in Rebecca's eyes, was a good thing.

I wrote a couple of Blueys a week to assure her she was in my thoughts constantly. Whilst I had started to calm down, the visit had shown me I needed to stop drifting and start to make concrete plans for our future.

Luc was extra attentive for the next week or two. We started to resume our romance and explored the many beautiful restaurants down cobbled side streets in out-of-the-way quieter districts away from the summer tourist traps that were full of wealthy Polish, German, and the emerging middle-class Russians.

'Smazchnego!' was commonly expressed when food was served, meaning 'good eating!' The canteen at my Language School served halc and hearty, cheap, nourishing food during the daytime. Luc and I would sometimes dine together for lunch if our schedules synched.

I still lagged behind Luc in my Polish language learning proficiency. I suppose once he arrived on the scene, I became a little lazy, and let him do all the talking. However, he was determined I was going to learn some language whilst we were together. I think the natural teacher in him saw me as a rogue student!

Luc used to write keywords and phrases on flashcards. They were all over his apartment! On every cupboard or object, there was a post-it note.

He was constantly getting me to read out and increase my vocabulary and for me to test him. He was very thorough and diligent. I was very lazy. I relied on personal charm, smiling and pointing with my finger at objects and hoping as soon as they heard my British accent, they'd immediately ask, 'Anglelski?'

"Er…tak, Anglelsku!" Nervous laugh.

"Oh Please, may we speak English, we love English, we speak, yes?"

This was a typical, often repeated pattern of conversation. Luc kept banging on about 'total immersion to absorb the culture'.

"Yeah, yeah Luc, but for heaven's sake, they have several ways of saying beer (Piwo) for christ-sakes!' I'd moan. 'It's such a difficult and exhausting language."

"Hey, honey, you're the one who wants to live here!" He'd retort.

CHAPTER 17

Chopin Festival

As summer matured into shimmering heat and humidity, we started to adopt an almost Mediterranean lifestyle. Early morning starts whilst the air was fresher, long leisurely lunches, quiet afternoons, then quicker action-packed evenings.

We had started to spend more and more time being exclusive and spending less socialising time with many colleagues. I started to spend days at his apartment in the former Jewish Ghetto district, about a twenty-minute walk from my apartment.

His block was in a low-rise concrete edifice, not quite as stylish as my block, in a quiet residential complex off Aleja Jana Pawla 11- One of the main arteries into the city running parallel with the River Vistula.

It was an easy route to follow to his block; I headed out of my apartment near the former Bank of Poland, walked alongside the Aleja Solidarnosci, then hung a right down the Aleja Jana Pawela 11 and took the first left until I reached a clinic. Luc's block was opposite along Zelaznia.

Two flights of stairs and a huge blue metal door with three locks guarded Luc like Fort Knox.

His apartment door was exceptionally thick. His apartment was about twice the size of mine but older, shabbier. It had a wonderful shaded concrete balcony with potted plants he couldn't kill - despite his total lack of green fingers. The balcony overlooked other non-descript housing complexes rather than the magnificent skyline my lounge window afforded.

It was lovely sitting out on a warm evening though, surrounded by some greenery and having a place to dry clothes naturally in the fresh air was a bonus.

There was an open-plan lounge diner with a well-equipped modern kitchen that was utterly wasted on Luc, as he wasn't a great cook.

He did, however, make magnificently towering sandwiches and introduced me to an American breakfast - the 'PJ' (Peanut Butter and Jam on toast).

He appreciated my attempts at home cooking; however, he often wouldn't eat a morsel until I'd cracked the pronunciation of the meal in Polish!

I gradually found out that Luc was a big prankster. He had a childish sense of humour and loved a good tale. He was an academic, and I suppose it was his way of decompressing his brain. Sometimes I appreciated it, but sometimes I was the butt of his jokes, which I didn't appreciate so much.

One evening he'd come home to find me hanging some laundry out on his balcony. I had my back to him, and I was warbling along to a tune on my Walkman headset, totally oblivious to the fact he had crept up behind me. Just as I was about to shake out some pillowcases and had my hands raised up, he slapped me on my bottom with a rolled-up newspaper.

I screamed so loudly, I think I could be heard across the city! My heart was thumping as I spun around and slapped Luc on his arm. Hard!

"Ouch! Hey! That hurt!" He said mockingly, nearly wetting his pants with laughter. "Oh my Gawd, the screaming! Wow! Honey! You're gonna give yourself a heart attack!" He guffawed. "I got you real good Ma'am!" He was almost crying at his own prank.

"I got you really WELL, you TWAT!" Not appreciating, that I had nearly toppled over the edge of his balcony.

I couldn't stay mad at him for too long.

We had fun, we hung out together, and we made love a lot. I suppose his apartment became a sort of 'love-nest'. For a few blissful weeks, there was no pressure; we just enjoyed getting to know each other.

We both enjoyed listening to classical music and would go to many concerts around the city. I remembered I'd bought tickets to the Chopin Festival in Lazienki Park when I first arrived in Warsaw.

The Royal Park is set in one of the loveliest, leafiest parts of the city. It's now the Diplomatic and Political Quarter with many beautiful Palaces and period buildings that weren't bombed in the War; consequently, it really hasn't altered much in a couple of hundred years.

Chopin is Poland's most celebrated composer and is hugely revered in Warsaw. So much so that a huge monument to him was erected in the park. It depicts Chopin sitting under a willow tree seeking inspiration from nature.

As soon as Luc and I approached the tram stop to Lazienki Park, you could hear faint strains of music. The tram passed beautiful rows of white-fronted 18th Century buildings; it was sizzling with heat that had built up during the day, and the area exuded a sense of wealth and grandeur.

As we approached the giant gilded park gates, our senses started to be stimulated. The glittering gates opened to reveal a long winding avenue of trees and small signs showing big arrows with a piano motif and the word 'Chopin'.

After a pleasant, gently sloping walk down to the lake in the middle of the park, we were met with officials in bright orange vests at a makeshift turnstile to check our tickets. We had the backs of our hands stamped with an image of Chopin; once we had been 'branded', we were free to roam about the park.

The Chopin Festival is only held every four years, so it was a fortunate fluke we had tickets to the event. An International piano recital of his complete works was to be played at the 'Theatre on the Island' in the middle of the lake.

Thousands of rose bushes surround the lake. It was an assault on the senses; the closer we approached, the heady perfume of the roses hit, in cloying accompaniment to the strains of the music.

As we turned a corner, we were met with a full frontal view of the 'Palace on the Water'. A beautiful building literally in the centre of the lake and attached to either side of the banking by a small pathway creating a moat effect. The moat separates, the auditorium from the stage, where a concert pianist sits on a raised dais with a ruined temple structure as a backdrop.

Listening to strains of lovely classical music, looking at the beautiful architecture and cooling shimmering water, combined with the increasing perfume of the roses at dusk, was simply, uniquely, magical.

It felt like a little piece of heaven on earth. It was seared into my memory.

Luc and I were transfixed. We'd brought a bottle of wine, a rug, bread and cheese. We'd settled down for our relaxed evening picnic in close union. Both absorbing, the beautiful vista and romantic atmosphere for at least an hour before Luc suddenly put his arm around my shoulders and said simply, "I love you Ellie. I really love you. Stay with me honey." His voice cracked with emotion.

"Oh Luc, I'm falling in love with you too. This is so perfect right now, isn't it? Wish we could stay like this forever, could there be any more perfect night than this?" I snuggled closer, feeling totally enveloped in our protective bubble.

The lights were switched on, and combined with the reflections across the lake, the rose bushes sort of glowed. The smell, the sounds, and the company combined to churn my emotions.

Was I truly in love? I'd only been in love once before, with Rebecca's dad - I did recognise some of the symptoms or was it just two lonely people clinging together in an unrealistic extended holiday romance?

At that precise moment, Luc turned to face me and said, "Marry me."

CHAPTER 18

Visa Dramas

I was reeling from Luc's proposal, completely blindsided.

We had just properly declared our love for each other, and I felt he'd got carried away and blurted out the 'M' word to follow!

I panicked; marriage? I'd come out to Poland to escape the death-rattle of the last marriage. I was only just clearing the dust from the new, bright, shiny, rehabilitated me. I was enjoying having choices again, doing what I wanted, having fun and romance, and taking time out from the crushing parental responsibilities of being a single parent.

I literally looked into his deep blue eyes for what seemed agonising hours, hardly breathing; my brain was rapidly computing my response so as not to offend his sincere proposal.

"Oh Luc, darling, Marriage? Wow! Marriage? Oh my god! Look, you know I've fallen in love with you, we've just said it to each other (nervous laugh), but marriage, well, that's a big, no, huge step Luc! (gulping) This is all a bit sudden, and I do thank you…. I love being with you, but, but, it's too soon for marriage. It's just too soon lovely."

Luc looked down, he was silent. He then looked up into the distance and broke away.

Nothing like a turned-down marriage proposal to burst the romantic bubble.

"Luc, Luc, please, can't we just enjoy this lovely evening? I AM in love with you; I love hanging out with you; you make me feel wonderful and cared for…Oh, say something?"

I gently linked my arm through his and kissed his cheek sweetly. He turned to face me silently and kissed me hard to cover his humiliation and to give him time to think of a response.

When he came up for air, he just 'shushed' me and put a finger to my lips as if to say no more words. Luc was naturally subdued for the rest of the evening.

I gave him the opportunity to come back to my apartment, but he made some excuse of catching up with his domestics. Neither of us wanted to dissect the conversation further.

It hung in the air, like smoke between us. I couldn't sleep a wink that night. My brain was whirring, and I was completely wired. I suddenly wanted to talk to my Mum. Some calm council, but the time difference stopped me from grabbing the phone.

Had I handled this properly? Would Luc brood about this and break up with me? How could just saying the words 'Will you marry me?' cause so much anxiety?

A wave of nausea and fatigue washed over me; I did need some sleep. I instinctively checked my phone for a goodnight text. No message on my phone.

No cheery 'You okay this morning hun? Xx', In the three months we'd been exclusively together, he'd not missed a beat. He'd always texted.

He's brooding, I thought.

As luck would have it, I was going to a teaching workshop that day about 'Handling Difficult Classroom Situations'. Oh, the irony!
It was interactive and had role-play situations. I was absorbed in the activities but equally kept checking my phone. Still no message. He was seriously brooding.

I was tempted to swing by his place after work; however, my pride wouldn't let me. I'd done nothing wrong, other than to clumsily tell him to cool it a bit.

Men! They're so frigging literal!

As I sat on the tram ride home to my apartment, I was getting increasingly grumpy about the scenario as I played it over in my head - the music, the lights, the setting, and the perfume of the roses wafting around like an aphrodisiac.

It was a romantic set up; he'd just got swept up. No big deal really. We were close, we could talk about these issues surely, like grown-ups.

As these thoughts were churning over in my mind and I approached the door, I didn't even notice a huge bunch of expensive florist flowers propped up against my doorway.

Not the weedy purloined bunches he regularly turned up with (he had a bad habit of yanking flowers out of the ground at parks to 'release' them for my pleasure!)

These flowers were gorgeous and had a card,

No stolen blooms this time. I'm a Jerk. I'm Sorry Ells. Luc xxx

I was genuinely thrilled at his attempt at peace-making. I soon put the blooms into vases, and the scent filled my small apartment with a heady perfume. I resolved to invite him over and left an answer phone message.

"Hello Luc, thanks for the flowers, they are really lovely…look, just wanted to say (pause)…er…sorry about yesterday. I'd really love it if you came over later. Just let me know. Love you."

I'd just started to make a brew when there was a knock at the door. I opened it to find Luc with one hand resting on the door, grinning sheepishly, sweating profusely and panting; he must have run from his apartment to mine.

"Sorry honey, I was deadbeat last night and forgot to charge my cellphone. I saw that you'd called. I slept like a log. I'm an idiot, but I thought you'd appreciate that I actually bought you some flowers, young lady and not swiped from Saski…Hey! Did you want some food? I've spent the afternoon cooking you a meal?" He said excitedly.

Luc cook? He never cooked. He assembled bits and bobs on the plate in various food groups, so he didn't starve, but he was no cook. Not wishing to kill the spirit of detente between us or his latent culinary skills that he may have hidden from me, I accepted graciously.

"Have you ever eaten Carp, Ells?"

"Hmm… It's fish, isn't it? The school secretaries mentioned they had it for their Easter meal." I replied hopefully.

"Yeah, I'd heard that too, so I went to the local market and bought some. Phoned up my Mom for a recipe."

Phoned his mum? Immediately the conversation I'd had with Marzena about him being a 'Mummy's Boy' came flooding back.

"Your Mum? Couldn't you have gotten it off one of the Polish staff?" I teased.

"Nah, Mom's a really great cook - I love her cooking; she gave me something real simple to follow."

"Well, let's face it, it would have to be simple if you're cooking it!" I laughed.

"Cheeky Miss! Now don't judge me just yet. Do you want some or not?"

"Go on then, I'll grab a bottle to go with it."

We decided to build up an appetite and walk back to his place. I imagined he would go all out with his prep and presentation in an attempt to heal over the little rift from yesterday.

We'd not mentioned the 'M' word, and I was guessing it had been taken off the agenda for the foreseeable. I wasn't expecting another proposal anytime soon.

When we arrived, I could smell the fish dish; the fishy waft was seeping out from under his doorway. Good luck getting rid of that smell, I thought.

Luc flung open the door confidently, "Hmmm smells great, doesn't it? Think next door's cat is gonna be eating plenty of fish…. I overdid the portion sizes!"

As predicted, he'd set out his dining table. Mismatched crockery and glassware, but he'd tried his best, and had found a tablecloth and attempted a flower display with purloined flowers in a milk jug.

The room's ambience was good, some soft jazz was playing on his CD player, and the mellow evening sun was shafting light into the room. He'd placed some fairy lights across his balcony and in some of the palm leaves in pots. It was a very inviting scene.

After five or so minutes, he swung by the kitchen busying with his dishes. There was a 'toot' sound as he announced the meal was to be served. He carried the lump of fish on a huge white platter to the table,

"Ta Dah! I give you Carp A La Lucas!"

"Hmmm…well, it smells okay, good start!" I joked. It looked hideous, a gelatinous mound with its boiled, beady eyes and gurning mouth looking out accusingly.

"Okay, just Okay? I've been slaving away for two hours lady!"

"What did you do to it then?"

"It's stuffed with herbs" (pronounced 'erbs, like Americans do), and breadcrumbs soaked in vodka and lemon."

"Nice, where's the rest of the accompaniments, you know, the other dishes?" I asked hopefully.

"What accompaniments?" He said. He was crestfallen. "What other dishes? We've got a lot of fish to eat!"

I couldn't help myself; I let out a huge belly laugh.

"Come round you said, I'll cook you dinner you said, not eat your own bodyweight-in-muddy-weirdly-looking-drowned-in-vodka-fish!" I roared.

To be fair, it tasted okay, but I made a mental note never to order it in a restaurant!

I always kept some sort of chocolate treat in my handbag, so we shared the chocolate bar as dessert and had coffee on his lovely balcony. We watched the last dregs of sun streak the darkening sky, and I let out a contented sigh.

"Awww, I loved that you went to all that effort darling." I said with genuine affection.

"Good, because I need to chat to you about something that's come up." He said sheepishly.

Immediately the atmosphere changed.

"What do you mean? Are you buttering me up for something here?" I asked.

"Buttering you up?" He responded quizzically.

"You know, breaking bad news, so stuffing me with fish first." I said, trying to keep it light-hearted.

"Oh I see. Oh no, not exactly."

"Oh c'mon Luc, what's up?"

"I've gotta go home to Massachusetts for a time - a couple of weeks, my uncle, Mom's brother passed, gotta go to the wake. You know we Irish-Americans are big on funerals, it's a family thing Ells." He said quietly whilst holding my hand.

"Oh, sorry to hear about your uncle; will your brothers be attending too?"

"Yeah, a gathering of the clan."

"When are you actually leaving?"

"In a day or two, as soon as Mom wires me some airfare, I can't afford it unless it's Apex."

"I can lend you something towards it if you want Luc." I offered.

"No, no…Mom understands; she's fine about it." He said, a little embarrassed. "What I also wanted to ask was if you'd move into the apartment, kinda look after the plants, next door's cat? You know I've kinda adopted it?"

"Move-in? As in, give up MY place?" I exclaimed wide-eyed.

"Well, I love you, I want us to be together; this is the perfect opportunity to move in, see how we get on, not pay two rents, you know? Sort of trial living together when I return." He said gently.

He was deadly serious. I suddenly sat up.

This was real life, rushing back and crowding out my bubble-of-fantasy romance.

Did I really love him or the idea of being in love? What did I really know of his character?

What I'd seen so far was good. He was clever, confident, funny, and kind to Rebecca when she visited, but he was also probably on his best behaviour and still wanting to impress me.

We hadn't seriously disagreed about anything to date, so maybe it was just the natural progression of our relationship to do a 'road-test'.

"I'll have to give my Landlord some notice Luc, but okay, let's do it!" I said, getting out of my chair and sitting on his lap, kissing him to seal the deal.

Luc visibly relaxed; we drank the rest of the wine and snuggled up on his comfy sofa in the apartment. I lay with my head in his lap, and he played and twirled with my hair in silence, just listening to the music.

It was as if we both recognised the shift in our relationship to something less frothy and carefree.

We were perhaps at the foothills of climbing a great invisible mountain of a relationship. We had lots of complications to navigate that I suddenly saw with great clarity, as I snuggled up next to him when we retired to bed.

"Visas!" I blurted out

"Visa's? What are you going on about Ells?" Said Luc sleepily.

"My Polish Visa expires at the end of my teaching contract in September. I HAVE to go back to London to get it renewed if I take up my new contract with the Language School…if I decide to return with Rebecca and settle over here."

"Oh, I see what you mean." Luc said, suddenly sitting up in bed wide awake. "Well, I was planning to go back to Mass when my contract finishes to carry on my research, then when I get my Doctorate, get a teaching post nearby to Mom, my contract finishes in December." He spoke quietly. "I'll be living with Mom on the horse farm till I get my doctorate."

"Horse farm?"

"Mom is a New England horse breeder and trainer of Morgan horses; we get people from all over the States wanting their mares covered by our studs. Lotta money in horses!" He giggled.

"Righto, so let me get this straight Luc, you've asked me to move into your apartment…even asked me to marry you, I recall, expecting me to trot back to America with you? What about Rebecca?" I said, swinging my legs out of the bed and grabbing a dressing gown.

"Hey honey, don't get all bent up about it; we're not married yet! I dunno Ells, hadn't thought that far ahead." Rubbing his head like he was about to get the mother of a headache soon. "I don't want to lose you! I don't want to lose this set-up between us."

I felt really claustrophobic at that point. I also desperately wanted my own space to be able to think.

I started to get dressed. Luc jumped out of bed. "Hey honey, c'mon, we're tired, let's just sleep and have a proper chat tomorrow, hey hey, shhhh, shhhh." He said, rubbing my back.

I reluctantly settled back, but I was wide awake. I suddenly realised all the really difficult conversations, I had to now line up with my daughter, my parents and Rebecca's dad about possibly emigrating to America.

Or could I walk away from this relationship? To others, it could be viewed as just an extended holiday fling.

I was computing the actual time I'd been with Luc, around four months. Not that long really for some heavy-weight life-changing decisions to be made.

But not tonight; I was exhausted and drifted off to sleep.

CHAPTER 19

Domestika

The following morning, the tension had evaporated, and we were back to the easy banter and closeness.

We had decided to have a proper 'chat' about everything when he returned from his family funeral. Luc's mum had sent a text overnight telling him the airfare money had been transferred.

By the time I'd popped out for some fresh rolls and milk, he'd already packed a light carry-on case. His best suit was in the US, so he was travelling light.

We talked through the logistics of his apartment. I resolved to half-move in. Not to put in my notice until we'd had the 'chat' on his return, but I would look after his place and move some 'girlie-stuff' in, keep the plants alive and feed the adopted cat.

The cat was a fat Persian that was probably pimping itself out to several residents. Luc had cats at his mother's horse farm. I suppose it reminded him of home to care for a pet.

"It's not your cat really Luc." I reminded him.

He pulled a sad face and said something crude about stroking pussies. He then gave instructions that under no circumstances was I to allow the plants to die, as his female landlord was most insistent they had to be looked after because they made the air healthy.

Actually, if Luc had dusted the leaves and cleaned six months' worth of dust, that might have been the case.

I didn't say anything to him, but like many bachelor pads, his apartment could have done with a deep clean and freshen-up. I knew what I'd be doing to while away the time waiting for him to return to me!

I accompanied him to Okencie Airport. Long farewell hugs and a tearful wave and promises to text every day. I saw him look back for a final wave before going off to board the great liner of the sky, a 747 Boeing to Boston Logan, Massachusetts.

Marzena came over to help me pack up most of my personal belongings in my apartment, and once we'd hauled a couple of suitcases over to his apartment, she offered to take me out for a drink at a bar she knew in the district.

"Fine, you lead the way Marzena, I have no idea where the bars are around here!" I laughed.

"I know a good local bar that serves Mead!" She exclaimed.

"Mead? Is that honey-based?"

"Yes, this bar does fantastic Dwojniak; it's half-honey, half-water, then fermented…very strong!" She glanced at me mischievously.

"I'll be drinking mead like a Monk." I giggled.

"You're no Monk…or Nun!" She howled with laughter.

The two-week plant and cat sitting passed uneventfully. I deep cleaned his apartment from top to toe; all the countertops were polished, cupboards rearranged, and corners and under the beds swept. The curtains were dry-cleaned, and a mountain of ironing pressed and hung up.

I also re-arranged his furniture to be more visually pleasing and logically flowing. I arranged and embedded my 'girl-crap' in the bedroom and bathroom.

After it had had the 'Ellie-touch' and new purchases of three scatter cushions, I felt like it was a lovely, cosy, love-nest. I'd hardly been back to my official apartment. It felt like a long goodbye to the space.

My small but very stylish central apartment, with views to die for, had walls covered in original art by the landlord's artistic son. I would spend ages tracing my fingers over the dimpled, grainy oil surfaces and paint topography. It fascinated me, the abstract shapes and smears. I really loved my own place, after sharing space with Rebecca, my parents and a marital home for several years and student digs before that.

I realised it had been the first space that was totally mine, and I was a little wistful. However, it had served its purpose as being a safe haven in the early days.

If Luc and I were going to make a success of our relationship, it had to be tested a little. We needed to spend time as a couple, doing the domestics together, seeing each other not at our best.

We were building that level of trust needed to progress a relationship rapidly as neither of us were in the first flush of youth, approaching middle-age. He'd had relationships before but not married or had children, although he had come close.

I still wasn't a hundred per cent sure what I wanted to do in life or who I'd choose as a life partner, but I was very clear what I didn't want.

I didn't want to be with a closed, unemotional man who could only give love metered out on their terms, often judging me physically. I didn't want to be with someone who couldn't talk to me openly. I didn't want to be with someone who had family that belittled me or thought that I wasn't good enough for their prince.

I just had to establish what Luc really wanted from me. I had a cryptic text message whilst he was away,

"Nothing can burst our bubble; miss the circle of love you and Rebecca can provide. I'm so grateful for the opportunity to step up to be a husband and stepdad. Didn't think I'd ever get the opportunity. LU xx"

That surprised me; Luc was an attractive man. I couldn't believe he'd never had the opportunity to really settle down. I didn't quite believe that I could be given the opportunity to find happiness again. I suppose both of us couldn't quite believe our luck.

Luc's face was a picture when he spotted me waiting for him at the Airport. I could see him scanning faces nearby. His face lit up with his megawatt smile, flashing those perfect teeth.

I tingled. The boy had 'it'. Sex appeal, in bucket loads.

His hair had grown a little and was looking curlier, glossier, with tiny silver flecks at his temples. He actually looked smart and classic in a blue poplin shirt; cuffs turned up showing tanned forearms, slim pressed Levi's and leather buckle belt, and matching leather Chelsea boots. He was dashing and healthy-looking.

I just wanted every inch of him!

We couldn't leave each other alone from the minute we embraced at the airport.

As soon as we entered the apartment, he was all over me, picking me up and flinging me onto the bed. He simply didn't register his apartment arrangements were different till much later as we lay exhausted, just melting into one another.

He got up to make some tea. Minutes later, he bellowed,

"WHERE THE HELL IS THE TEA CADDY? Where is everything?" He laughed as he staggered back into the bedroom, clutching only a teapot.

"Do you know how damned sexy you look just carrying that?" I giggled. "Are you using THAT to stir the tea?" I smirked.

"BEHAVE YOU HUSSY! Honestly, where's the damned tea Ells, Seriously?"

"In the logical place? The cupboard above the kettle!"

"Oh, you're the logical one now, huh?"

I heard him opening and closing various cupboards, muttering to himself.

"Oh Honey, love what you've done to the place…even those scatter CUSHIONS!" He shouted from the kitchen.

"GOOD! Took me ages to buff this place up to my standards!" I retorted

He returned with a tea tray, bearing a teapot, two cups and breakfast buns. He carefully placed it on the tallboy chest of drawers, turned around and climbed back into bed.

"And now young lady, I'm going to buff you up to my standards!" He laughed as he slipped between the sheets.

The tea was forgotten about for ages.

We fell into a rhythm of living together that worked for us both. Yes, we had the odd tiff over minor irritations, usually when we were both tired, or if I was hormonal.

I quickly learned that Luc was a voracious reader, he devoured knowledge, and when he was writing up his research, he got into his 'zone'.

His face became quite serious with concentration. His reading glasses made him look like the fictional character Clarke Kent, his Superman power was to scan-read. He could absorb so much information very quickly.

He had to have silence though. No radio. No birdsong. No chatter. Just silence when he was working. He could be easily irritated by extraneous noises and would shut himself into a hermetically sealed space by shutting all doors and windows.

I loved birds tweeting morning greetings; I loved the city thrumming and pulsating with life. Strains of conversation, music, the chatter of school kids. I enjoyed all the summer sounds of life.

So, as I was an early bird, I would make my coffee and go to the balcony, which was really comfortable and not sticky at 6 am. That was my 'alone' time, my thinking time before the madness of the working day and the sticky heat drained me.

Apart from these idiosyncrasies, we rubbed along pretty well together. After a few more weeks, we emerged from our 'bubble' and started to socialise more with school colleagues and his sister Lisa, and invited several around for dinner parties. We were often teased as 'love-birds'.

As the summer matured, we attempted to get out of the city more by taking little day trips on the Polish rail system.

Trips out to Krakow and Poznan were memorable. We often got the wrong trains at the wrong times. Even Luc's superior language skills didn't save us sometimes; it was hilarious. If it had just been me, I could have headed off to Ukraine or Lithuania!

So when the light started to turn mellow and golden towards the end of summer and my school contract was looming to a close, the elephant-in-the-room had to be addressed, and we had to have a proper chat about our futures.

The past few weeks since his return from the States had been wonderful; an oasis of calm, sexual healing, friendship, fun, laughter, and deeper trust between us.

Could I honestly give that up? Close this chapter of my life with no regrets?

I felt like I was in love. I cared about him. I missed him when he wasn't around. I just wanted to share everything with him.

It was time for the big 'talk' about our options if we were to stay together.

I decided to make a delicious meal before I broached the topic. Firstly, to make sure Luc was in a mellow mood and in a space where we could open up and honestly talk. That was impossible in a restaurant, however, discrete.

The evening was perfect, it was the last weekend in August, and the humidity and stifling heat had died down. He'd enjoyed my cooking, and we were now drinking my expertly made espresso martinis out on his now verdant and twinkling balcony.

"Luc, can we talk?" I ventured.

Luc took a breath, he knew what was coming. He'd absolutely NOT mentioned the 'M' word again since the evening of the Chopin Festival.

It felt like talking about it again would jinx the lovely experiences we'd had and burst the bubble-of-freedom we'd created between us.

"Sure darlin."

"Well, you know I care about you, and we've been getting on famously, it's been so happy for me this time together, but I've got to make some decisions here Luc. I just double-checked my contract today. I've got just less than four weeks teaching time left, then I have to leave the country." I paused for breath; Luc was looking out over the balcony. "I'd like you to visit my family back in the UK and spend time with me and Rebecca. Can you do that?" I said, my voice cracking.

Luc rocked back into his chair and took a deep intake of breath.

"Man! Oh Thank God! I was so scared you were going to quit us! YES! yes, of course, silly…Yes, I'd love to meet your Mom and Dad and spend time with Rebecca, she's such a lovely little girl." He got up and pulled me to him, smothering me with lots of kisses.

"So, you'll come out for a week when I return to the UK? I wouldn't want you to get to know Rebecca better unless I wanted to be with you, you understand?" I cried.

"Ellie, I want to be with you. I want to marry you; everything else is just detail baby." He smothered my mouth with a long passionate kiss, and all discussion ended.

CHAPTER 20

Details

In the final weeks, Luc started to open up about more intimate details of his life in the US. Sharing is caring, I believe. He was starting to trust me with understanding his lifestyle in Massachusetts.

He lived with his mother, in a beautiful New England 'Colonial' clapperboard homestead, after living out in California for five years in a previous relationship.

It was a historic building that had been in his family for generations and stood on hundreds of acres of forest in a rural idyll of a region in New England called 'The Berkshires'. Although Luc was at pains to make sure I knew he wasn't rich himself, he was basically an academic and wanted to be a public school teacher, not a captain of industry or businessman like his elder brother.

His mother had basically run through her inheritance and family fortune running the horse farm. There were fifteen horses and three nationally recognised stud horses at the farm. Another farm at the Connecticut property with ten horses and a family holiday home up in Vermont that the extended family all used.

He showed me photographs of his favourite paddock behind the farm where family (another sister lived in the same village) would hang out and have campfires. I could see why he wanted to return home to his roots.

I finally put my notice in with my Landlord. I was quitting to return to the UK soon anyway, and I returned to my apartment one last time to collect some clothes and the large suitcase I had arrived in Warsaw with on that coach several months ago in the depths of winter, alone, cold, nervous. It seemed like another life.

I'd arrived in Poland, stripped of my assets, save a few precious belongings, photo frames with snapshots of Rebecca and my parents. I had jettisoned, my previous unhappy and shattered life and set off on an adventure with an open mind but a bruised heart.

I hadn't given up hope of being happier and finding love again, or what I'd understood to be love. If I wasn't fully in love with Luc, as some people define it, it was definitely lust, transitioning into caring. Love is something deeper, and I felt the faint tendrils of it stitching my fractured heart back together.

There were many details to sort out, i's to dot and t's to cross.

The first task being the ruddy visas and let's not forget that both of us would have huge hoops to jump through with stiff immigration rules on both sides of the pond!

To be able to work in Poland in the late 1990s, before they joined the EU, you had to obtain a Work Visa from London with a letter of employment. They were a nominal price but were issued six months at a time. You had to return to the UK before applying for extensions or further Visas.

I had planned to do my first six months, establish myself with work, set up an apartment, and make arrangements for schooling my daughter (the language school would have helped with that).

I'd really enjoyed the Polish way of life; although a Catholic country, religion was not 'sold' to you; it was interwoven into the social fabric. Poles are very family orientated, and I was welcomed into my Polish colleagues' homes and holiday homes as part of their extended family

I loved the definite seasons, foods to look forward to eating that were ripe to buy; food that was hale and hearty, not overprocessed and faddy. I loved the culture, the arts, the Polish work ethic, music, cinema and the avant-guard architecture.

In short, I developed a real love affair with Warsaw, and I'd been making foundational plans to rebuild and settle in this country with Rebecca. I'd fully intended to return home after six months and say to my family, 'Yes, it's all set up. This is the plan. Let's go!'

Meeting Lucas, put a great big spanner in the works and complicated my choices no end. Of course, my parents had known about him in passing references and in conversations.

"Oh how's your nice American chap? Lucas? How's he doing?" My Mum would ask.

I'm sure Rebecca had been pumped for information about Mummy's New Boyfriend as soon as she had returned after her brief visit. My Mum could easily wheedle nuggets of classified information; she'd missed her calling as an MI5 Agent and never missed a trick at putting two and two together.

"So, he's not been married or got kids? Is he gay?" She'd say casually.

"No Mother! He's definitely not gay!"

"But he lives with his mother over there, does he?" She said in a slightly judgemental tone.

"It's not a crime to be a loving son either, Mum; by all accounts, it's a big property with a lot of land and plenty of horses!"

"Right, so when are we meeting Mr Wonderful then?" She giggled.

"He's coming over soon, probably before his new semester in September."

"Righto, well, your Dad and I are going away on holiday for a week on around the fifth, okay? So you can work around that, can't you?"

Each day, I could feel the tension grow about the return visit back to the UK. Not least from the Language School, which wanted a firm commitment from me for the new student semester.

I simply stalled

My Plan A had changed, and I didn't want to sign something that didn't fit in with my new situation with Luc. If I signed a new contract, I'd be out in Poland with Rebecca attempting a new life alone again.

Luc had made it very plain. He wanted to marry me and return to the US eventually with both me and Rebecca. He had a well-established teaching post back in Massachusetts and had his home with his mother.

My options were to return to the UK, back to Rebecca without Luc. Get a job teaching in British schools or private tutoring and live with my parents until I scraped enough cash to find us a home.

Another option was to return home temporarily to the UK and prepare Rebecca and myself to jump through the Visa and Immigration process to the US. Enter the US on a Fiancé Visa and establish a life in Massachusetts living with Luc in his family home.

Or return to Poland, sign a new contract and establish a new life with Rebecca in Warsaw, but ultimately apart from Luc when he returned to the US.

All three options came with a hefty dose of reality.

The Status Quo was the bubble of freedom Luc and I had currently, but that was ultimately unsustainable without my daughter.

My retired parents, had put their own lives on hold to help raise my girl. They did it out of love. She loved them, and it cemented a close bond that was precious. However, it was understood by all parties to be temporary, not forever.

So I stalled, and stalled, and stalled. I simply avoided the meetings and necessary paperwork with the Language School. I'd left a message with the secretaries to forward any mail or documents to my parents' address back in the UK, and I'd confirm before the end of September when the new teaching semester would start.

I'm a great procrastinator. I simply needed more time to think through my options, and I certainly needed to talk through my options with my family, Rebecca herself and, more importantly, Rebecca's father.

Rebecca's dad had rights. I could foresee an issue if he refused to let me live in the US with his only daughter. He was within his rights to refuse to let me take her out of the UK. I knew he was going to be unhappy about the situation. This was not a meeting I could have over Skype.

All of these details were crowding in on me; suddenly, I felt an overwhelming desire to return to England. To everything that I knew and understood.

In reality, of course, life had moved on. Rebecca was growing up. My Ex was dating again and had found himself in a new relationship. The home I had shared with my Ex had finally been sold in the UK. Even back home wasn't the same.

I had to put some breathing space between Lucas and me to put our relationship into context and to test it a little. To see if it could withstand the loops of bureaucracy, the questions and scrutiny of family and my Ex.

How was I going to support myself as an immigrant in a foreign country? Would I be living in Massachusetts with his mother? Or would Luc use this as an opportunity to establish his own home and independence? What was schooling like for Rebecca?

Questions, questions, questions!

Our final couple of days seemed morose. Luc had started to become quiet, subdued and contemplative. I think he was feeling the weight of the realities of life too. Our love-nest situation was ending, and our choices were in the balance.

As I started to pack my huge case, I realised I was compartmentalising my life. I was closing the case on this wonderful experience. What would be the result of opening the case and exposing this time away to family scrutiny?

On the taxi ride to Okencie Airport, Luc held my hand and hardly said a word for fear of us both breaking down. It was an ending of sorts.

I was never going to be living in that apartment again. We'd made it our safe haven and had filled it with caresses, laughter, life and now love.

I was going home to face the music, but hoped Luc would charm my family and Ex when he visited. It was still all a risk. We could both return to our home countries and have a change of heart. I had to take the risk and trust him at his word.

Trust a man. It was time I did.

Looking out of the taxi window as we sped ever closer to Okencie down Marszalkowske, a wide thoroughfare, zooming past some of the beautiful historic, period buildings, out towards the city limits, I said a silent goodbye to Warsaw.

Would I ever return to take up a new contract in a place that had accepted me and shown me nothing but adventure and life, so vivid and in such stark contrast to back home in Britain?

Could my heart take returning, but knowing I would definitely have to say goodbye to Luc, unless we married and returned together to the US?

Did I really, really want to get married again?

Was I completely over Rebecca's dad?

Did I want to emigrate to America?

I was a maelstrom of emotions but mostly of gratitude for having this single time, as a gift, from my loving parents. For being a mother, it gave me purpose and drive to achieve for Rebecca's sake.

At the airport, as the final minutes clicked away waiting for me to board my BA Flight to Heathrow, Luc suddenly turned to me, held me close and said quietly,

"I really love you Ellie; you don't know how much meeting you has excited me, made me want to get on with life again after drifting since I returned from California. I'm coming over to visit you and your family and have a man-to-man chat with your Ex."

Burying his head into my neck and then kissing me for so long, not wishing for the moment to end. 'You've got me; I love you, only you.' His voice cracked with emotion.

As I trudged away toward the departure gate, my stomach grew tight with anxiety as I didn't enjoy flying, and my emotions were off the scale.

I'll never regret making the break from my tired and washed-up life back in the UK.

I'd come alive again as a newly confident, sentient, creative woman. I was thirty-six, and I had transformed my look and my outlook. I was not the same Ellie. I had been changed by this formative experience.

I turned to see him wipe a tear and smile such a smile as to seal our fate and lock out all resistance.

It's all in the details now, I thought, Just details.

Conclusion

The Polish LOT Airlines flight to London, Heathrow, gave me plenty of time to think about my first trip to Poland.

Remembering the wintery departure to the Continent earlier in the year, the cheery view of the white cliffs at Dover and the nervous anticipation of a change of lifestyle to come.

I knew instinctively that I had to take some risks and chances at living a life unknown to me. I knew I'd be scared and challenged; that's how you grow as a person.

That I survived, found my feet, and actually flourished as the Warsaw weather became more benign, gave me an enormous emotional boost.

As I started my adventure, I'd carried so much guilt and shame inside me over the failure of my first marriage. Although it takes two, doesn't it? I was always made to feel like I carried the can for its ultimate disintegration.

As the large. 747 BA flight gathered momentum, my stomach lurched as we took off back home to face the music. To settle down, to make some really important life-changing decisions for myself and my daughter.

However, I'd done something the naysayers hadn't thought I'd be brave enough to follow through with or indeed contemplate doing for themselves in their own lives.

The look on Luc's face at the Airport told me all I needed to know to keep the faith between us. He'd fallen in love with me, and I with him. It was that simple and that complicated.

However tricky, the next few months were going to be to actually establish a new life together, the immigration hurdles we'd have to jump through, introductions to family on both sides of the Atlantic, getting my finances in order, preparing Rebecca for yet more upheaval in her young life. None of it was going to be as hard as having the conversation with Rebecca's father.

I was effectively planning to take his beloved, only daughter out of the country. It was high risk. He had rights, and if he'd flatly said no outright, that pretty much would have been it as far as my relationship with Luc could have taken us. We couldn't do long-distance; it wasn't feasible. He didn't want to settle in the UK because of his family commitments. I also respected my Ex to abide by his decision. He was her father. I had loved him once, and I wouldn't just deprive him of seeing his daughter regularly without his approval. He had been a good dad.

So all of this was floating in my head, as I flew into Heathrow. I caught the train connections to travel home to see my parents and Rebecca.

Yes, I had to tidy up all of those details, but I was picking up lines of new beginnings; for the first time in a couple of years, I had hope, expectation and excitement in my life. Such a stark contrast to the heartbreak, sadness, and anxiety before.

Would this new love last? How does anyone know that at the start? I had to trust in hope. Hope is so unquantifiable and unmeasurable.

The moment I stepped over the threshold of my parents' home, my darling girl rushed up to me. As I swooped her up, she showered me with many soft kisses, and there were many tears from both of us.

I knew I was hopeful, alive, and shining with love.

Love for my parents, who'd sacrificed their time for the love of their grandchild. Love of my country, even though I'd loved exploring another. Allowing new love into my life with another man, but most importantly, I had fallen in love with myself again.

I loved that my spirit of adventure had been rewarded and that my creativity and hope had been renewed and refreshed. I was ready for whatever path I needed to travel with Rebecca.

A new life awaited.

About the Author

Ellie is a 'Posh Girl'. The colloquialism given to those born in the city of Peterborough. She studied Civil Engineering at Aston University before swapping to a Business degree. A successful career within the Construction Industry. An Overseas career as a TEFL teacher and several years in mainstream teaching in

England with a final relocation to Cumbria to concentrate on her writing and establishing her Writing Retreat, Hearten House. Ellie is now happily married. She is a Mother and Grandmother and lives in a historic Cumbrian town.

'Cowboys & Cocktails' Is her first memoir.

A fantastic way to keep in touch with Ellie:
www.littleredtypewriter.co.uk
https://www.facebook.com/EllieAuthorBooks

Printed in Great Britain
by Amazon